Gay and Lesbian Identity:
A Sociological Analysis

THE REYNOLDS SERIES IN SOCIOLOGY

Larry T. Reynolds, *Editor*

by **GENERAL HALL, INC.**

Gay and Lesbian Identity:
A Sociological Analysis

Richard R. Troiden
Miami University
Oxford, Ohio

GENERAL HALL, INC.
Publishers
5 Talon Way
Dix Hills, New York 11746

Gay and Lesbian Identity:
A Sociological Analysis

GENERAL HALL, INC.
5 Talon Way
Dix Hills, New York 11746

Copyright © 1988 by General Hall, Inc.

Publisher: Ravi Mehra
Composition: *Graphics Division,* General Hall, Inc.

LIBRARY OF CONGRESS CATALOG CARD NUMBER: **87-82056**

ISBN: 0-930390-79-2 [paper]
0-930390-80-6 [cloth]

Manufactured in the United States of America

To Muriel Pomasel Troiden and Wayne Lee Benjamin

Contents

6 The Identity-Construct Approach 80

7 The Essentialist Model 101

8 Conclusion 123

Appendix
The Risks of Sex Education and Research 130

Environment 142, Institutional Goals 143, Why Remain? A Personal
View 143

Acknowledgments

I would like to take this opportunity to acknowledge the people whose social, intellectual, and emotional support made this book possible. Thanks are due to members of the gay and lesbian community. Their willingness to be observed and interviewed has improved the quality of research and theorizing on homosexuality. I owe an enormous intellectual debt to Vivienne C. Cass, John H. Gagnon, Erich Goode, Gregory P. Stone, Kenneth Plummer, and William Simon. Their ideas shaped the theoretical framework of this book. I would also like to thank Barry D. Adam, Robert C. Atchley, Martin P. Levine, Kay Phillips, Mildred P. Seltzer, Linda Singer, Larry T. Reynolds, and Theodore C. Wagenaar for their comments and criticisms of earlier drafts of this manuscript, and Karen Feinberg and Irene Glynn for their editorial assistance. I am also grateful to Ken Brahms, Len Dupras, Sandy Roll Evans, Judy Blexrud Hachey, Gayle Troiden Morgan, Walt Pridemore, Don Roberts, Rollin Shove, and Sally Taylor, M.D. for their unflagging support and encouragement. A special thanks goes to Russ and Marge Troiden for their love, friendship, and respect.

Three portions of this book are revised versions of material that appeared elsewhere. Chapter 3, "Self, Self-Concept, Identity, and Homosexual Identity," is a revised version of "Self, Self-Concept, Identity, and Homosexual Identity: Constructs in Need of Definition and Differentiation," which appeared in *Journal of Homosexuality* 10 (1984/1985). Chapter 4, "A Model of Homosexual Identity Formation," is a revised version of "The Formation of Homosexual Identities," which will appear in *Journal of Homosexuality* 16 (1988). The Appendix, "The Risks of Sex Education and Research," is a revised version of "Walking the Line: The Personal and Professional Risks of Sex Education and Research," which appeared in *Teaching Sociology* 15 (1987).

Richard R. Troiden
Miami University (Ohio)
January, 1988

Chapter 1 INTRODUCTION

Gay and Lesbian Identity has two major themes: (1) sexual conduct is primarily social; and (2) professional thinking about sexuality in general, and homosexuality and homosexual identity in particular, is undergoing constant change. In the United States, societywide shifts in conceptions of sexuality and gender have been associated with changes in professional perceptions of homosexuals.

As a sociologist, I find sociological concepts extremely useful in both my professional and my personal life. Concepts or ideas drawn from sociology provide me with a broader basis for understanding social life than ideas I have encountered in the related disciplines of psychiatry and psychology.

Traditionally, concepts drawn from psychology and psychiatry have dominated informed discussions of homosexuality. The professional literature virtually lacks a unified and empirically grounded approach to homosexual identity from a sociological perspective. Although sociologists have long been interested in various aspects of homosexuality and have frequently investigated its various dimensions, they have made few attempts to integrate these theoretical and empirical observations with the emerging research literature on homosexual identity. A goal of this book is to demonstrate the contribution that sociology makes to an understanding of homosexuality, and particularly of homosexual identity formation.

Major Themes

Over the past fifteen years, research into homosexuality has undergone a major shift in emphasis. A concern with documenting the etiology, treatment, and psychological adjustment of homosexuals has been replaced by an interest in understanding how homosexuals themselves perceive and experience the homosexual situation in contemporary Western society. The issue of *how* a person develops a homosexual identity—an organized perception of self as homosexual in relation to sexual and romantic settings—has only recently commanded the attention of social scientists.

People are not born with perceptions of themselves as homosexual, ambisexual (bisexual), or heterosexual. Before they can identify themselves

1

in terms of a social condition or category, they must learn that a social category representing the activity or feelings exists (e.g., homosexual preferences or homosexual behavior); discover that other people occupy the social category (e.g., homosexuals exist as a group); and perceive that their own socially constructed needs and interests are more similar to those of persons who occupy that social category than they are different. In addition, they must begin to identify with those included in the social category; decide that they qualify for membership in the social category on the basis of activities and feelings in various settings; elect to label themselves in terms of the social category (i.e., define themselves as "being" the social category in contexts where category membership is relevant); and incorporate and absorb these situationally linked identities into their self-concepts over time (Lofland 1969; McCall and Simmons 1966; Simmons 1965).

The outcome of these subjective processes is an *identity transformation,* a change in self-perceived sexual orientation from heterosexual or bisexual to homosexual. A heterosexual or ambisexual perception of self in relation to sexual and romantic settings is replaced with a homosexual perception. Becoming homosexual involves the formation of homosexual self-perceptions and the decision to adopt homosexuality as a way of life (Plummer 1975). Becoming homosexual is a form of adult resocialization; that is, it involves adopting an identity and way of life that represent a radical departure from previous socialization experiences.

Because this book focuses on women and men who become homosexual, I am not concerned with the origins of homosexuality, that is, with what causes an individual to develop an erotic preference for the same sex in the first place. Whether sexual orientations are established before birth (Bell, Weinberg, and Hammersmith 1981a; Whitam and Mathy 1986), determined before age nine (Harry 1982), or organized out of experiences gained with gender roles and their related sexual scripts (Gagnon and Simon 1973; Plummer 1975), the *meanings* of sexual feelings are neither self-evident nor translated directly into consciousness. People *construct* their sexual feelings to the extent that they use systems of sexual meanings articulated by the wider culture to interpret, define, and make sense of their erotic yearnings. Becoming homosexual involves the evolution of a homosexual identity, a perception that one *is* homosexual in relation to romantic and sexual settings, and a decision to adopt a corresponding lifestyle.

The theoretical approach adopted here is symbolic interactionism, a social-psychological perspective within the discipline of sociology. From an interactionist perspective, the link between sexual activities and sexual identity is *problematic:* Homosexual activities or feelings do not necessarily crystallize in perceptions of self as homosexual; conversely, a homosexual identity is not necessarily the outcome of homosexual activities. Not all women and men who engage in homosexual activities, entertain homosexual fantasies, or have homosexual preferences become homosexual in the sense that they perceive themselves as homosexual in the romantic and sexual sense. Certain contexts and experiences, which are described in the following chapters, facilitate or hinder the evolution of homosexual identities.

Gay and Lesbian Identity is the first book to differentiate analytically the constructs of self, self-concept, identity, and homosexual identity within a unified theoretical framework. With the exception of Vivienne Cass's work (1983/1984), these conceptual distinctions have not been drawn in previous discussions of homosexual identity, and this lack of distinction has contributed to conceptual disarray (Troiden 1984/1985).

During the past twelve years, several investigators have developed theoretical models that describe the process by which homosexual identities are acquired. These models were constructed using accounts provided by homosexuals themselves (Cass 1979, 1984; Coleman 1982; Lee 1977; Minton and McDonald 1983/1984; Plummer 1975; Ponse 1978; Schäfer 1976; Troiden 1977, 1979; Weinberg 1977, 1978).

Gay and Lesbian Identity develops an ideal-typical model of homosexual identity formation that represents a synthesis of, and elaboration on, previous theorizing and research on the subject. The model developed here is unique in four major ways: (1) It is grounded in current research and theory; (2) it describes identity formation in both lesbians and gay males; (3) it notes similarities as well as differences between the sexes in homosexual identity development; and (4) it explains differences between gay males and lesbians in terms of their experiences with gender-role socialization.

Theorists disagree sharply about the nature and meaning of homosexual identities. Do homosexual identities represent a confusion of being with doing, the mistaken belief that one is what one does, the equation of the entire self with one form of behavior? Do homosexual identities represent one of several major interests constructed socially and defined as reflecting essential facets of personality? Are homosexual identities inevitable, unambiguous outgrowths of a specific kind of sexual orientation present at birth, the outcroppings of an essential, inherent, and inescapable facet of personality? Much of this book is devoted to a discussion and integration of these competing perspectives.

The works and ideas of professionals — academic or not — are influenced and shaped in numerous ways by the prevailing social and intellectual climate. The growing emphasis on applied technical skills in the wider society has been mirrored in academia, where importance is attached increasingly to the applicability of knowledge. Today, more frequently than in the past, one hears the question, "Will the research yield results that can be applied in real-life settings?" Unfortunately, "facts" do not speak for themselves. They must be interpreted, which is why concepts are so important and useful. Concepts are like the lenses in glasses: They help people see and understand their social worlds more clearly. Sociological concepts incorporated in the text illuminate the complex issues involved in disciplined attempts at understanding homosexuality and homosexual identity.

Plan of the Book

This introductory chapter has defined the issues that *Gay and Lesbian Identity* addresses and has outlined the unique features of the book. Chapter 2 presents a sociological approach to sexual development and homosexuality. Chapter 3 differentiates the constructs of self, self-concept, identity, and homosexual identity within the framework of symbolic interactionism. Chapter 4 defines ideal types, reviews the literature on homosexual identity formation, and presents an ideal-typical model of homosexual identity formation in lesbians and gay males. Chapters 5, 6, and 7 describe, analyze, and integrate three competing perspectives on homosexual identity: the social-role approach, the identity-construct perspective, and the essentialist model. The text concludes with a synthesis of these three perspectives. The Appendix describes the personal and professional risks associated with careers in sex education and research in academic settings.

Chapter **2** SEXUAL DEVELOPMENT
AND HOMOSEXUALITY

An interactionist perspective on human sexuality emphasizes the social
sources of sexual conduct, or the role of social and cultural forces in shaping sexuality and guiding its expression. This chapter begins by discussing
ideas that appear commonly in discussions of sexual development from the
perspective of symbolic interactionism: polymorphous perversity, human
sexualities, sexual scripts, and sexual socialization. The latter portion of the
chapter, which concerns homosexuality, likens the acquisition of homosexual
identities to a status passage, views homosexuality as consisting of multiple
dimensions, defines the term *homosexual,* notes the problematic link between sexual identities and sexual behaviors, discusses the incidence of
homosexual behavior, and provides a typology of homosexuality.

Polymorphous Perversity

From the viewpoint of symbolic interactionism, people are born in a
state of *polymorphous perversity,* an open-ended, diffuse, and relatively
fluid capacity for bodily pleasure seeking that may attach itself to any of the
objects, people, or events that exist in the immediate culture. Everyone is
born with a capacity for a wide range of sexual experiences, including the
potential for both masculine and feminine behavior. This capacity is
capable of being diffused among many objects and being expressed for
multiple reasons (Foucault 1979; Gagnon 1977; Gagnon and Simon 1973;
Hart and Richardson 1981; Plummer 1975, 1981b, 1984; Simon and
Gagnon 1984).

Sexual preferences develop out of this flexible pleasure-seeking potential.
These preferences are organized and directed socially as people learn about
and experiment with the sexual scripts made available to them by their
culture. Experiences gained in social, genital, and emotional realms shape
and direct the original, diffuse pleasure-seeking tendency into *sexual
preferences* — organized systems of sexual meanings that channel sexual
desire. To quote Hocquenghem (1978):

> Desire emerges in a multiple form, where components are only
> divisible *a posteriori,* according to how we manipulate it. Just

5

like heterosexual desire, homosexual desire is an arbitrarily
frozen frame in an unbroken and polyvocal flux. (p. 36)

Human Sexualities

John Gagnon (1977) prefers the term "human sexualities" to "human
sexuality" because the former captures more effectively the diverse and
pluralistic nature of sexual feelings and expression:

> The choice of the plural centers on my belief that there are many
> ways to become, to be, to act, to feel sexual. There is no one
> human sexuality, but rather a wide variety of sexualities. Had it
> been possible, I would have made the word "Human" plural as
> well. Just as there are many sexualities, there are many
> humanities, different ways of being sexual, different ways of
> being human. (p. i)

Although human beings mature and develop biologically in a rather
orderly sequence, the psychological meanings that adhere to these
developmental changes are not fixed or eternal. Cultures vary enormously
in the meanings they attach to the processes of human development. These
sexual scripts, rather than nature or biology, shape and guide sexual conduct.

Sexual Scripts

The domain of meaning and conduct referred to as sexuality is ac-
cumulated through social learning. That is to say, sexual conduct is
primarily social in origin (Gagnon 1977; Gagnon and Simon 1973; Plummer 1975; Simon and Gagnon 1984). Existing sociocultural arrangements
define what sexuality is, the purposes it serves, its manner of expression,
and what it means to be sexual.

People learn to be sexual much as they learn everything else. The polymorphous perversity with which women and men are born is guided and expressed through *sexual scripts*. Sexual scripts are sets of norms, values, and
sanctions that govern the erotic acts, statuses, and roles recognized among a
social group (Laws and Schwartz 1977). These scripts are learned and
organized during adolescence along lines previously laid down during
gender-role socialization. Males, for example, are taught to see sexuality in
active, genitally focused, and goal-oriented terms; females are encouraged
to view sexuality in reactive, emotionally focused, and process-oriented
ways (Laws and Schwartz 1977; Levine 1987).

Sexual scripts are articulated by the wider culture and resemble blueprints; they channel and focus sexual conduct by providing sexuality with its affective and cognitive limits (Gagnon and Simon 1973; Simon and Gagnon 1984). These scripts provide sexuality with its *affective* or emotional boundaries by specifying what kinds of feelings are sexual. "The mind has to define something as 'sexual' before it is sexual in its consequences" (Plummer 1975, 30).

Sexual scripts also designate the *cognitive* borders of sexuality by indicating appropriate and inappropriate partners (the *who*), proper and improper sexual behavior (the *what*), acceptable and unacceptable times for sex (the *when*), permissible and nonpermissible settings for sex (the *where*), positively and negatively sanctioned motives for sex (the *why*), and appropriate and inappropriate sexual techniques (the *how*) (Gagnon 1977; Gagnon and Simon 1973; Simon and Gagnon 1984). This is not to deny a biological substratum to sexuality but to emphasize the powerful role of social forces in shaping sexual conduct. Because sexual learning occurs within specific historical eras and sociocultural settings, sexual conduct and its meanings vary through history and among cultures.

Sexual scripts exist at three analytically distinct levels: *cultural scenarios, interpersonal scripts,* and *intrapsychic scripts* (Simon and Gagnon 1984). Cultural scenarios are official and public, and are reflected in religion, law, media, folklore, and legend. In contemporary America, sociocultural arrangements articulate three somewhat different cultural scenarios: *procreative, relational,* and *recreational* (DeLamater 1981, 266).

Procreative scripts present sexuality as subordinate to procreation. Only sexual activities related directly to procreation are legitimized. Nonprocreative options—masturbation, cunnilingus, fellatio, anal intercourse, and homosexual relations—are condemned. Relational scripts prohibit sexual expression outside committed relationships, which may or may not involve marriage, and present sexual activity as a "means of expressing and reinforcing emotional and psychological intimacy" (DeLamater 1981, 266). Nonprocreative options are viewed as legitimate, provided both partners agree to them. Recreational scripts define mutual pleasure, sexual release, or both as the primary purpose(s) of sexual activity and legitimize sexual conduct between mutually interested partners even if they are perfect strangers. These scripts permit any mutually agreed-upon acts that enhance erotic pleasure. A person's social class and biological sex often determine the scenario he or she is encouraged to adopt.

Sexual scripts at the interpersonal level, influenced heavily by cultural scenarios, represent a person's understanding of what is expected of her or him in situations defined as sexual or the range of identities and roles available to the self and others as sexual actors. An individual's expectations and wishes regarding sexuality and sexual expression are also components of interpersonal scripts.

Intrapsychic scripts create sexual fantasy and provide people with the motives to act in ways defined culturally as sexual. Intrapsychic scripts evolve as people internally rehearse (fantasize about) reality "in ways to more fully realize the actor's many layered and sometimes multi-voiced wishes" (Simon and Gagnon 1984, 53). In short, intrapsychic scripts function to elicit and sustain sexual arousal.

Situational constraints and partners with different intrapsychic and interpersonal scripts create the need for accommodation, a negotiation process that must result in a mutually acceptable script if a sexual exchange is to occur.

Sexual Socialization

Learning sexual scripts is a complex process because of its experiential nature, because of the indirect and unclear fashion in which adults transmit sexual information to the young, and because children generally acquire sexual information or misinformation from peers in clandestine settings. Sexual scripts are learned during adolescence and flow along contours already mapped by gender-role socialization.

On the experiential side, Gagnon and Simon (1973) assert that an essential ingredient in psychosexual development is learning to identify the kinds of feelings that the proximate culture defines as indicating states of sexual arousal. The ability to make sense of one's sexuality, however, presupposes a certain level of verbal sophistication. The beginnings of sexual awareness are

> observable in young adolescents when they are required to learn what the feelings they have with reference to early post-pubertal sexual arousal "mean." Events variously categorized as anxiety, nausea, fear are reported which are later finally categorized as (or dismissed, even though they still occur) sexual excitement. (Gagnon and Simon 1973, 21)

Adults often hinder sexual learning through their unwillingness to discuss sexual topics. More often than not, they adopt one of two responses to a child's use of words or displays of activity that other adults would define as sexual.

> He may *mislabel* the behavior, describing it as something it may not be, or *non-label* the behavior by ignoring or providing a

judgment without a specific label. (Gagnon and Simon 1973, 32; italics added)

The tendency to judge without naming is especially prominent. If the sexual activity is named, moral labels, such as "dirty" or "bad," rather than understandable sexual terms, are often attached to the behavior. The dilemma faced by youngsters, then, is learning to attach

> the proper words to proper feelings and acts. The possession of words, experiences, and judgments, all unassembled, leaves the child without a vocabulary with which to describe his emerging physical or psychic experiences. (Gagnon and Simon 1973, 39)

The inability or unwillingness of most adults to convey sexual information clearly to the young encourages children to turn to peers for sexual information and misinformation. Although what is learned is important, Gagnon and Simon (1973) maintain that the contexts in which the young acquire sexual information is even more important:

> The exchange of sexual information among children is clandestine and subversive, and the manner in which parents attempt to teach their children reinforces this learning structure. The admonitions of parents since they are general and diffuse, do not result so much in cessation of either interest or behavior, but in their concealment and the provoking of guilt. (p. 40)

On its broadest level, the clandestine atmosphere surrounding the acquisition of sexual information affects how people learn to manage their sexualities. It explains partially how people — regardless of sex and sexual orientation — come to see sex as a private matter, something to be concealed from prying eyes. Moreover, the subterranean and furtive fashion in which sexual information is acquired encourages people to invest sexual matters with the mantle of the forbidden as well as the private. To learn about sex in America is to learn about guilt. Similarly, learning to manage sexuality entails learning to deal with guilt (Gagnon and Simon 1973).

At the end of childhood, girls and boys have an imprecise understanding of erotic practices; they possess a bundle of fragmented, disconnected knowledge, none of which has been assembled in a way that is personally meaningful. They may know, for example, that babies come out of a woman, but are confused about the mechanics of sexual intercourse and reproduction. Physical acts in the sexual sphere become meaningful only when embedded in sexual scripts, which are acquired during adolescence.

In adolescence, sexual experience is tacked on to information already acquired about masculinity, femininity, and sexuality.

> Moral categories and oppositions (good and evil, purity and degradation, modesty) and gender role activities (aggression and submission, control and freedom, needs for achievement and affiliation) are integrated into scripts, at first private, then collective, which contain new meanings to be applied to organs, activities, and people which make up the conventional sociosexual drama. (Gagnon and Simon 1973, 53)

Sexual scripts are fleshed out in two sequential phases. The first phase occurs during early adolescence, between ages eleven and sixteen; the second stage takes place in middle to late adolescence, from ages sixteen to eighteen (Gagnon and Simon 1973, 101).

Early Adolescence

Information acquired during early adolescence shapes the meanings that boys and girls place on their pubescent erotic development, particularly the bodily changes and feelings that accompany their budding adult sexual responsiveness. (Most adult differences between the sexes in sexual attitude and behavior originate during this period.) Families and schools, for the most part, avoid teaching boys and girls how to interpret and respond to their emerging sexual capabilities. To gain instruction in how to be sexual, the young are forced to rely on their peers, and, to a lesser extent, on the media.

At first, same-sex peers teach each other about the activities associated with their emerging sexual capacities. Because males and females receive quite different messages about the management of their emerging sexualities, they are here discussed separately.

Girls. In early adolescence, girls learn to fuse sexuality with femininity and emotionality. Sexuality, femininity, and emotionality are connected because girls are socialized to adopt procreative, and, in some cases, relational sexual scripts. Mothers, female relatives and teachers, and other girls teach girls to be womanly (i.e., seductive, submissive, nonaggressive, and physically attractive) in erotic interactions. These audiences also encourage young women to acquire the relationship skills necessary for intimate relationships: emotional disclosure, expressiveness, and an ideology of romantic love (Laws and Schwartz 1977; Levine 1987; Tavris and Wade 1984). Those instructed to adopt procreative codes learn that certain noncoital activities (e.g., kissing, touching, perhaps even petting) are legitimate in intimate relationships but that coitus is to be reserved for marriage. Those who are taught relational scripts learn that sexual intercourse is also permissible in committed, love-based unions.

Socialization agents rarely teach young women recreational codes. Indeed, girls are warned of the dangers of adopting recreational scripts — the risks of contracting sexually transmitted diseases, of becoming pregnant out of wedlock, and of damaging their reputations as "nice girls" — that could render them unsuitable for meaningful dating and marital relationships. (Because of the herpes and AIDS epidemics, adults and teen-agers of both sexes are now cautioned widely and wisely against recreational scripts.)

Girls, unlike boys, are not encouraged to be sexual or recognize their feelings as such. Whereas an erect penis is easy to interpret as a sign of sexual arousal, the signs of female arousal are less easy to identify in the absence of sexual experience (Tavris and Wade 1984). Consequently it is easier for girls to ignore their genitals and remain ignorant of them. Girls are also less likely than boys to discover and practice masturbation, let alone talk about it, because it receives little, if any, support from female peers.

Boys. By contrast, earlier experiences with the masculine gender role lead boys to perceive the sexual realm as one more arena in which to demonstrate their masculine competence.

> Taught that men are knowledgeable, they strive to become proficient at erotic acts. Having learned that men are aggressive and dominating, they learn to initiate and direct sexual conduct. Knowing that men are achievement-oriented, they make [sexual behavior] goal-oriented, with conquest and orgasm the measures of success. Realizing that men are competitive, they pit their performance of sexual acts against other males. And lastly, taught that men are independent and individualistic, they divorce sexual activities from emotionally binding relationships. (Levine 1987, 38)

An increase in male hormones during puberty causes boys to have frequent erections, even in the absence of erotic thoughts or activities, which focus their attention on their genitals. Peer support, as well as their hormonally induced, heightened sexual responsiveness, reinforces young males in their first attempts at achieving sexual competence — the practice of masturbation. Because procreative sexual scripts define both sexual desire and masturbation as moral wrongs, however, boys typically view their masturbatory activities with mixed feelings. Often guilty and ashamed, they masturbate in private, away from adult eyes, and disclose their activity only to peers, if to anyone at all (Levine 1987).

Masculine gender-role training, however, influences even the practice of masturbation. "Knowing that sex occurs in private, recognizing that men are independent, take the initiative, and strive for success, youth for the most part masturbate alone, at their own discretion, and until they climax" (Levine 1987, 39-40). Experience with male sex roles also guides the content of their masturbatory fantasies, in which they assume the role of the active, directive partner.

Boys' masturbatory patterns teach them to view sex in a detached, privatized, phallocentric, and objectified fashion (Levine 1987). Because masturbation is detached from emotional relationships, the practice creates and reinforces the idea that the primary motive for sex is erotic release. Sexuality comes to be defined as highly personal, since masturbation takes place in private and involves only self and self-gratification. Men also learn to favor sexual acts that stimulate the genitals, since masturbation focuses on genital manipulation. Moreover, the fantasies that accompany masturbation center on physical attributes—breasts, vaginas, legs; therefore, imaginary partners are reduced to sex objects. The emphasis on physical acts deflects attention from the imaginary partner's psychological characteristics, which remain uneroticized (Levine 1987).

Young men consequently acquire sexual scripts that typically link sexual expression with recreation. Erotic activity is divorced from intimate relationships and procreation, and is equated instead with physical pleasure. Exactly the opposite situation characterizes the socialization of young women, who learn to link sexual expression only with relationships or procreative endeavors.

Middle and Late Adolescence

In middle and late adolescence, young men attempt to expand the range of their sexual experiences beyond solitary masturbation, kissing, and petting. Because they have learned to divorce sexuality from intimacy, they search initially for young women from whom they can obtain more advanced sexual experiences—sexual intercourse, cunnilingus, fellatio. In the process of expanding their sociosexual repertoires (e.g., dating, going steady, being engaged) they acquire the skills necessary to manage adult sociosexual relationships. Young women who were taught to equate sexuality with intimacy, commitment, and marriage refuse these overtures; only "bad girls" have casual sex.

Adolescent dating offers women and men opportunities to improve their social status, as well as chances to obtain sexual gratification. Adolescent males regard dating, going steady, and sexual conquest as demonstrations of masculine prowess. Among teenaged females, dating and going steady validate femininity by serving as proof of their desirability, physical attractiveness, and marriageability (Levine 1987).

Boys find themselves in a socially precarious situation at this point in their lives. Because adolescent culture stigmatizes permanent relationships with "bad girls"—they are fine for sex, but unacceptable for relationships—boys must become *emotionally* involved with "good girls" to gain peer status, something they have scarcely been taught to do. Girls find themselves in precisely the opposite situation. They must permit some level of *sexual* involvement in their relationships, something for which they have received little or no training.

The final phase of a young man's sexual socialization is obtained through his relationships with "nice girls." Young men begin to learn the language of dating and courtship through their dating interactions with "respectable" young women. The experience of sexuality within the context of intimacy encourages young men to incorporate relational elements into their sexual scripts—elements that equate sexual expression with commitment and emotional intimacy—along with the recreational components they learned earlier. Young women, in contrast, learn about the physical side of sexuality through their dating interactions with young men and begin to incorporate recreational elements into the procreative or relational scripts they have already acquired.

By the end of adolescence, young women and men have acquired fully the sexual scripts that will organize and guide their adult sexual patterns, although males are somewhat more familiar and comfortable with the physical dimensions of sexuality, and females are more familiar and comfortable with the intimate side of relationships and the ideology of romantic love. The content of these gender-based sexual scripts remains more or less unchanged throughout life, although it may be modified later to fit with life-cycle situations such as motherhood, fatherhood, middle age, and old age (Tavris and Wade 1984).

Homosexuality as Status Passage

Not all girls and boys fit the pattern described above. Some, aware of their same-sex attractions since early adolescence, avoid heterosexual structures and do not develop the competencies associated with their gender until they are older (Bell, Weinberg, and Hammersmith 1981a; Saghir and Robins 1973). Others yield to parental and peer pressures (Bell, Weinberg, and Hammersmith 1981a; Harry and DeVall 1978) and participate in heterosexual rating, dating, and mating scenes; but homosexual desires and fantasies prevent them from integrating these experiences psychologically.

They perceive the behaviors as unsatisfying and at odds with their genuine natures (Levine 1987).

The sociosexual situation encountered by adolescent lesbians and gay males is often quite different, then, from the sexual socialization encountered by heterosexuals. Key properties of the status passage to homosexuality as a way of life often deprive adolescent lesbians and gay males of opportunities to learn, rehearse, and practice the sexual scripts that will govern their adult sexual patterns. Their sexual socialization typically begins only when they have made contact with the homosexual subculture, which occurs most often at or after late adolescence. This issue is discussed further in Chapter 4.

A *status passage* refers to observable changes in identity and world view that accompany movement from one social position to another. Defining the self as homosexual and adopting a corresponding lifestyle involves a change in social status from that of (presumed) heterosexual to homosexual. Several key properties mark the passage to homosexuality: isolation, lack of clarity of signs, centrality, undesirability, and irreversibility (Plummer 1975).

The early stages of this passage occur in relative *isolation.* The stigma surrounding homosexuality usually prevents prehomosexuals from discussing their emerging feelings, desires, and concerns with parents and peers. Partly for this reason, identity confusion is a common feature during the initial stages of homosexual identity formation (Cass 1979, 1984; Dank 1971; Plummer 1975; Troiden 1977, 1979). The identity confusion experienced by adolescent lesbians and gay males is discussed at length in Chapter 4.

A *lack of clarity of signs* is another characteristic of the passage to homosexuality, largely because clear behavioral signs indicating homosexual inclinations do not exist. Gender-inappropriate interests or behaviors during childhood, for example, do not *necessarily* prefigure adult homosexual patterns. The same may be said for a relative lack of sexual interest in the opposite sex or sexual attractions for the same sex. The emotional states that feelings signify are neither self-evident nor unambiguous, and the meanings of emotions are notoriously hard to pin down. People affix labels to their feelings by trial and error, as a consequence of reflecting upon the significance and the meanings carried by their activities and the associated feelings.

In view of the cultural link between homosexuality and gender-inappropriate behavior, and because of the lack of legitimacy accorded bisexual options in America, the presence of these characteristics makes it easier for people with homosexual inclinations to acknowledge the tendencies once they gain accurate information about homosexuality. Conversely, the absence of homosexually associated traits makes it more difficult for people to perceive homosexual propensities in themselves (Troiden and

Goode 1980; Warren 1974). These ideas are elaborated more fully in Chapter 4.

Centrality is a third property of the status passage to homosexuality as a way of life. From a conventional perspective, and from the vantage point of many homosexuals, homosexual status is thought to be a defining characteristic of self, an outgrowth of deep-rooted needs that intrude upon, or are implicated in, nearly all situations and interactions.

In America, a commitment to homosexual lifestyles is also regarded widely as *undesirable*. At best, homosexuality is presented as a sexual "variation" or an "alternative sexual lifestyle." At worst, homosexual congress is seen as the willful activity of the "utterly immoral" and the "depraved." Between the two extremes lies yet another interpretation: Homosexuality is seen as a "sickness" and the homosexual as a "victim," crippled by a condition over which she or he has no control.

Finally, a commitment to homosexuality as a way of life is seen as permanent and *irreversible*. Once developed, sexual orientations are viewed as fixed and unchanging. People treat their sexual orientations and sexual identities as stable and immutable; the idea that they may be flexible and subject to change represents a serious threat to their experience of social reality, their view of both self and others, and the ways they relate to others, especially those of the same sex (Hill 1980).

A Multidimensional View of Homosexuality

Homosexuality in males and females occurs on a heterosexuality-homosexuality continuum that ranges from a minimal to a predominant or exclusive sexual interest (attraction) and/or contact with members of the same sex. The research of Kinsey and his associates (1948, 1953) verified the existence of a heterosexual-homosexual continuum. These investigators rated adult sexual attractions and behavior using a 7-point scale with 0 (zero) for individuals with a history of exclusive heterosexuality; 1 through 5 for individuals with a history of varying combinations of heterosexual and homosexual desires and experience, a higher score indicating a higher degree of homosexuality; and 6 for persons with a history of exclusive homosexuality both in overt sexual behavior and in covert responses and erotic interests. On this scale, individuals rated 3 show no dominant sexual preference. Persons at the level of 3 are often referred to as bisexuals.

To do justice to the complexity of human sexualities, it is useful to conceive of human sexual patterns as involving a number of dimensions in addition to sexual behavior and sexual attraction, especially if one's purpose is to classify people as heterosexual, bisexual, or homosexual (Goode and Troiden 1974). The dimensions of sexuality included in such analyses are often, but not always, intertwined. Analyses that ignore the numerous dimensions, however, or focus on only a few, obscure the complexity of human sexualities.

People may be homosexual, heterosexual, or bisexual according to some dimensions but not according to others. The dimensions of sexuality along which people may vary are sexual behavior, sexual attraction, sexual fantasy, sexual identity, romantic (emotional) preference, social preference (i.e., male or female company), and lifestyle pattern, such as homosexual, heterosexual, or bisexual (Goode and Troiden 1974; Klein, Sepekoff, and Wolf 1985). On any of these dimensions, people will range along a continuum. Those who fall at the extremes might be classified for descriptive purposes as exclusively heterosexual or homosexual in that specific dimension, while individuals whose feelings or behavior are more moderate might be described as bisexual or ambisexual.

Definition of Homosexual

From an interactionist perspective, the term *homosexual* involves more than a certain kind of sexual orientation or sexual behavior. It also encompasses an identity and a way of life.

> The dropping of the mask, the putting on of the true identity, the ritual celebration of brotherhood [and sisterhood] enhanced by stigma and secrecy, and the sexuality experienced within this world of meanings. (Adam 1978a, 13)

In this book, *homosexual* refers to people who define themselves as such and adopt corresponding lifestyles. People who fit this description typically classify themselves as homosexual along most of the dimensions listed in the previous section. As defined here, *homosexual* is synonymous with *committed homosexual,* a term encountered again in the typology of homosexuality at the end of this chapter.

Problematics of Activity and Identity

The relationship between homosexual activity and homosexual identity is neither fixed nor absolute; a certain amount of independence exists between sexual behavior and sexual identity. Women or men may define themselves as homosexual without the benefit of homosexual experience. Studies of homosexually responsive people who marry heterosexual partners indicate that some people define themselves as homosexual without ever having engaged in homosexual behavior (Coleman 1985a; Dank 1972; Ross 1971, 1972). For these people, fantasized sexual encounters involving the same sex generated homosexual perceptions of self. This finding suggests that individuals may develop sexual identities even in the absence of the overt sexual behaviors normally linked to the identity. Thus connection need not exist between *subjective* categories and the external acts thought to represent them.

Conversely, people may engage in overt behaviors thought to express specific sexual identities without possessing the corresponding identities. That is, homosexual behavior is not necessarily an expression of a homosexual identity. Women and men may engage in homosexual acts without developing perceptions of themselves as homosexual. Recent evidence indicates that large numbers of adult males in the United States (Coleman 1985b; Delph 1979; Humphreys 1970; Ponte 1974; Troiden 1974) and abroad (Whitam and Mathy 1986), and many American teenaged boys with lower-class, urban backgrounds (Hoffman 1972; Reiss 1964) engage in homosexual behavior but do not consider themselves homosexual. Sexual acts may be compartmentalized subjectively to leave unaffected an individual's sexual identity. *Objective* behaviors need not correspond to the internal categories thought to generate them. The typology of homosexuality developed at the end of this chapter encompasses these observations.

Incidence of Homosexual Behavior

Research reporting the incidence of homosexuality in America and elsewhere is flawed in at least two major ways. First, it usually focuses only on the dimensions of sexual behavior and/or attraction, which does violence to the multidimensional nature of homosexuality. Second, the representativeness of the people who take part in such research is questionable. Therefore the figures reported below should be treated as incomplete and suspect.

At some point between adolescence and old age, many men and women have sexual relations with a person of their own sex. Kinsey's data from the 1940s and 1950s and Morton Hunt's data from the early 1970s indicate that at least 25 percent of American men have one or more homosexual experiences to orgasm after the onset of adolescence. The corresponding figure for women is 15 percent (Hunt 1974; Kinsey et al. 1948, 1953).

Of those men and women who give homosexuality a try, even fewer decide to repeat the activity with the same or different partners. Only about 3 to 4 percent of American males and 1 to 2 percent of American females beyond the age of fifteen identify themselves as exclusively homosexual, that is, as never having had a heterosexual attraction or sexual experience (Hunt 1974, 303-19; Kinsey et al. 1948, 610-66; Kinsey et al. 1953, 446-501).

A Typology of Homosexuality

One way to capture the variety of forms assumed by homosexuality in contemporary America is to classify the behavior along some of its dimensions. I categorize homosexually experienced women and men according to the degree to which their homosexual behavior is socially organized, interpreted as homosexual, and perceived as significant.

By "socially organized" I mean the degree to which organized group structures, such as groups and subcultures, support and legitimize homosexual behavior and its expression. By "interpreted as homosexual" I mean the ways in which women or men view their sexual episodes (anticipated or real) with the same sex and the meanings they attribute to the behavior. By "perceived as significant" I mean to specify whether men and women perceive their homosexual conduct as meaningful enough to warrant defining themselves as homosexual. Plummer (1975, 99) has developed a similar typology.

As mentioned earlier, statistics on the incidence of homosexual activity indicate that most people with homosexual experiences limit their encounters to a few isolated episodes. In these contexts, the behavior is not defined as homosexual, nor do participants see it as representing a central life concern and self-identity. Nor does the activity occur as part of an ongoing and organized erotic system, such as a homosexual bar. Instead, the behavior is set aside or abandoned soon after it is sampled, and it is defined as reflecting something other than homosexual interests. A sexual episode involving another woman or man may be written off as an experiment, a lapse of judgment, a result of drug intoxication, a good thing to do at the time, an alternative sexual outlet, a change of sexual pace, a phase of development, or a manifestation of bisexuality. The spontaneous decision of two teenaged boys to masturbate mutually or experiment with fellatio, or an infatuation between two adolescent girls that results in kissing and petting to orgasm, provide examples of *ambiguous homosexuality:* The activity falls outside organized homosexual group structures that maintain and sustain lesbian or gay sexuality. Moreover, the participants do not interpret the behavior as homosexual, nor does it generate perceptions of self as homosexual.

For other women and men, homosexuality assumes a different form: It is something to be kept hidden, acknowledged but pushed to the periphery of everyday concerns. Men and women who practice *clandestine homosexuality* view their homosexual behavior as expressing a fundamental emotional need and typically define themselves as homosexual or bisexual. They regard or interpret their sexual activity as homosexual, but do not involve themselves actively in the more open and public facets of the homosexual subculture, such as homosexual friendship networks, bars, shops, and restaurants.

A woman who adopts a clandestine homosexual style may live publicly as heterosexual, involve herself with the opposite sex at varying levels of intimacy, and avoid public places where lesbians are reputed to gather. At the same time, she may be deeply involved in a discreet love relationship with another woman, which she defines as a special, never-to-be-repeated event.

In contrast, a man who practices clandestine homosexuality is more likely to immerse himself in the more loosely organized and less visible sexual systems that emerge in out-of-the-way public places. He may establish anonymous and impersonal homosexual liaisons with other men in public restrooms, YMCAs, public parks, highway rest areas, movie theaters, and public beaches rumored to be homosexually active. Sexual release is achieved quickly and easily, with no expectation of commitment beyond the moment (Delph 1979; Humphreys 1970; Ponte 1974; Troiden 1974).

Situational homosexuality is a third possible form of homosexual expression. This style emerges typically in three settings: (1) same-sex environments, such as prisons and the armed forces, where sexual contacts with the opposite sex are limited or impossible; (2) working-class neighborhoods in large urban areas, where male adolescent peers see "hustling" homosexuals for profit as acceptable; and (3) cultures such as the Latin American, North African, and Asian, which define sexual relations with males as an acceptable secondary sexual outlet (Whitam and Mathy 1986). In these three settings, group structures emerge to legitimize homosexual expression as long as it occurs in a highly circumscribed fashion. Same-sex contact is not regarded as homosexual as long as certain conditions hold.

In same-sex environments, sexual relations with the same sex are not usually seen as homosexual if the participants announce heterosexual identities upon entering the setting and maintain ties with the opposite sex outside the institution. Incarcerated females, for example, almost always use terms other than "homosexual" to describe the romantic and sexual pairing that occurs in women's correctional institutions:

> Some of the argot terms reported by previous investigators are *girl-stuff, playing, being together, the doll racket, chickvot relationships, having people, making it, trying in, and bulldogging.* (Propper 1978, 266)

The general condition of sexual deprivation that characterizes life in same-sex institutions is used to legitimize experimentation with alternative sexual patterns or the outright sexual exploitation of the same sex (Davis 1972; Heffernan 1972; Propper 1978; Ward and Kassebaum 1968; Wooden and Parker 1981). In some cases, the homosexual behavior represents a pattern imported into prison life. In other cases, homosexual liaisons emerge in response to the general conditions of sexual deprivation (Propper 1978). In principle, only the latter pattern represents situational homosexuality.

Norms legitimizing circumscribed homosexual activity also exist in the subterranean world of male prostitution ("hustling"). Neither the hustler nor his peers view his sexual contacts with other males as homosexual as long as he has a girlfriend, undertakes homosexual activity only for money, adopts the inserter role during homosexual encounters, does not reciprocate sexually, remains emotionally cold and distant throughout the encounter, and abandons the activity when he is old enough to find legitimate work (Hoffman 1972; Reiss 1964).

In parts of Latin America, Asia, and North Africa, it is acceptable to use male homosexuals — especially as passive partners in anal intercourse — to supplement heterosexual outlets as long there is no emotional involvement (Whitam and Mathy 1986). Although organized group patterns support situational homosexuality, the behavior rarely brings about changes in identity (from heterosexual to homosexual) and is generally not defined or treated as a bona fide instance of homosexuality.

Committed homosexuality represents the deepest level of involvement with homosexuality as a way of life. Committed homosexuals perceive themselves as homosexual in relation to sexual and romantic settings and adopt corresponding lifestyles. They accept themselves as homosexual and are comfortable with the homosexual identity and role, which they see as expressing valid, deep-rooted emotional and sexual needs.

People vary, of course, in the degree to which they structure their lives to accommodate their homosexual identities and roles (Humphreys and Miller 1980). Women and men who work in the corporate world, which is known to take a dim view of homosexuals and their lifestyles, find their working hours peopled primarily or entirely by heterosexuals. For these men and women, homosexual companionship is relegated to the back burner of their lives and reserved for periods of leisure. In other instances, people may choose to enter an occupation known to tolerate homosexuals (e.g., the arts) or to leave one kind of work (e.g., teaching school) for a kind situated in a more accepting milieu (e.g., counseling).

Individuals may also immerse themselves completely in the homosexual subculture, move to a gay ghetto in a major city such as New York, take a job in a homosexually owned business or develop such a business themselves, eat at gay restaurants, buy in homosexually owned shops, and make the rounds of local bars and establishments that cater to a homosexual clientele. Committed homosexuals may also become gay activists and devote a good portion of their time and energy to the homosexual struggle for human rights. Or they may adopt apolitical postures and decide to live quietly and unobtrusively with their lovers in a suburban subdivision or a gentrified inner-city neighborhood.

Despite different levels of involvement, committed homosexuality differs in focus and meaning from the other adaptations discussed in this chapter. The participants desire and seek love, sex, and companionship from members of the same sex. They recognize these needs as important and value them for themselves.

Chapter	**3**	SELF, SELF-CONCEPT, IDENTITY,
		AND HOMOSEXUAL IDENTITY

The constructs of self, self-concept, identity, and homosexual identity are elusive and difficult to define without reference to some sort of theoretical framework (Maslow 1968). To provide a reference point for the reader, the conceptualizations developed in this chapter are shaped by the sociological perspective of symbolic interactionism and are consistent with that perspective.

The social-psychological literature contains few analyses of the relationship between self and identity. As Cass (1983/1984) notes, some investigators use the constructs interchangeably, others differentiate between the two, and still others see identity as a component of self. A similar lack of conceptual differentiation characterizes the literature on homosexual identity formation, which contains only two analyses of the relationship between the constructs of self and identity (Cass 1983/1984; Troiden 1984/1985).

To understand homosexual identity it is necessary first to understand the general concepts of self, self-concept, and identity. Accordingly, this chapter begins with definitions and descriptions of these concepts and proceeds to a discussion of homosexual identity.

Constructs

Self and identity are *constructs*. Constructs are defined as

> concepts devised to aid in scientific analysis and generalization. They are generally inferred indirectly from observable phenomena. They are abstractions from reality, selecting and focusing on certain aspects of reality and ignoring others. They are *heuristic assumptions* designed to guide and suggest fruitful areas of investigation; they are not intended as a direct description of concrete phenomena. (Theodorson and Theodorson 1969, 74)

Constructs have a number of characteristics: They are ideas; they are general; they represent whole classes of phenomena; they are themselves abstractions; and their existence is generally inferred indirectly from observable phenomena.

Cognitions, affects, and needs are examples of constructs. They cannot be observed directly because they occur within the body or mind; their internal, subjective status is apparent in the way they are defined conventionally. *Cognitions* refer to the process of knowing, including both awareness and judgment. *Affects* are strong emotional responses considered apart from the bodily changes they produce. *Needs* are physiological or psychological requirements necessary for the well-being of an organism.

The existence of constructs must be inferred from overt behavior or characteristics because the phenomena to which they refer are intangibles that cannot be assessed directly by empirical means. Self and identity, like cognitions, affects, and needs, are constructs because they are subjective and cannot be measured or observed directly.

I have organized my discussion of the relationships among self, self-concept, identity, and homosexual identity by describing and analyzing the dimensions and components contained in each construct. A *dimension* is the sum of logically related components associated with an idea or object (Sedlack and Stanley 1984), in this instance, with the construct "self." Self-esteem, for example — feelings of like or dislike in relation to self — provides an *affective* dimension of the objective self. Self-image, in contrast, is contained within the *cognitive* dimension of the objective self. The term *component* (attribute or subset) refers to a constituent part or specific characteristic associated with a definable and self-contained entity (Sedlack and Stanley 1984). A component is incorporated within a larger dimension; shame and pride, for example, are components or subsets of the affective or feeling dimension of the objective self.

Self

In the most general sense, self is an individual's consciousness of his or her own being. Consciousness of being is achieved in part when one can respond to oneself socially as an object in the same fashion that one responds to other people as social objects (Meltzer 1967, 9). In more formal terms, *self* is an organized set of relatively consistent and enduring conceptual responses that serve to regulate other responses of the same individual (Lindesmith and Strauss 1956).

Self differs from *personality* in that the latter generally refers to "the dynamic organization within the individual of those psychophysical systems that determine his characteristic behavior and thought" (Allport 1961, 28). A focus on self invites consideration of subjective phenomena — thoughts and attitudes — as they relate to self-indication or a view of oneself as a social object. Personality, in contrast, invites consideration of how self-indications are translated into "organized sets of persistent and characteristic patterns of individual behavior" (Stone and Farberman 1970a, 367).

Contemporary formulations of self originate in the conception developed by William James (1892). For James, the self was reflexive; it was apprehended as both knower and known, subject and object, "I" and "me." He treated the "I" and the "me" as "discriminated aspects," or different phases of self-reflection, not as separate things or components. One aspect cannot be understood without reference to the other. James viewed the "I" aspect (self as knower) as corresponding to "pure ego" (subjective self), and labeled the "me" aspect (self as known) as the "empirical ego" (objective self). The "I" and the "me" were seen as discriminated aspects, as different phases, of the cognitive dimension of self.

George Herbert Mead (1934) elaborated the distinction between the "I" and the "me." For Mead, the "I" was the aspect of self that represented an individual's response to the attitudes of others. The "me" was the aspect of self that reflected upon the responses of others to the earlier, "I"-initiated action. That is, the "me" was a composite view of self abstracted from experience and acquired while the individual tried out the specific roles of particular persons in the immediate social group. Self-reflection, in turn, altered the previously held conception of self—the "me"—and gave rise to a new "I." The "I" propelled the "me," setting the stage for further evolution of self.

A *role* is an expected pattern of behavior associated with a social *status* or position in the social structure. Role taking is subjective; it occurs in the individual's mind before or instead of objective, concrete action. The subjective process of role taking involves a person's perceptions, conceptions, communications, and actions in regard to herself or himself. These judgments and perceptions grow out of interactions with *significant others* —persons with whom an individual's most important interactions occur.

The "me" also contains the *generalized other:* "the generalized role or standpoint from which the individual views himself and his behavior" (Meltzer 1967, 11). The generalized other, commonly referred to as the "conscience," is the perspective of the wider community; it forms an individual's moral awareness. As part of the "me," according to Mead, the generalized other regulates and shapes conduct, and grows out of interactions with significant others. The judgments and opinions rendered by important others about the self are not necessarily embraced uncritically and *internalized,* that is, incorporated into the self as a basis and impetus for future actions. Instead, argued Mead, individuals test against reality the image of self obtained from the generalized other; in turn, reality modifies the view of self obtained from others.

As implied above, Mead's view of self stresses the cognitive dimension. Cooley's (1902) idea of "self-feeling" builds on James's (1892) notion of "self-esteem" and fleshes out Meadian analysis by introducing the affective dimension of self—feeling, mood, or sentiment. For the interactionist, then, self is entirely social in origin and emerges through symbolic interaction or communication.

Yet self does not operate in a subjective vacuum; it is linked to needs, which it channels and directs. Some needs are grounded in biology, programmed into the species, present at birth to one degree or another. The needs for food, air, and bodily contact are ready examples. Other needs originate in the social realm and emerge from interactions with people who share a similar culture; the desires for approval, success, popularity, and achievement serve as examples.

People are also predisposed to develop in certain ways, and these potentials may be either inherited (right-handedness) or learned (a sense of being masculine or feminine). A predisposition, such as artistic ability, intelligence, or athletic prowess, may be realized if the immediate environment is conducive—that is, reinforces the pattern—and if the individual sees the condition or activity as meaningful and rewarding. In contrast, if the person or the immediate social group fails to reward, recognize, or attach significance to the potential, it may remain dormant.

Although needs and predispositions form the physiological and psychological core of the individual, the developing "me" shapes an individual's responses to these needs and thus contributes to his or her conception of self. Needs do not translate themselves directly into consciousness, let alone activity; they must be interpreted before they can be acted upon.

When people develop the ability to manipulate symbols, especially words, they learn to isolate and distinguish among feelings. Language allows them to make fine discriminations among internal states. Socialization and self-development help individuals learn which words symbolize rage, love, sexual arousal, or sadness. Without the aid of language, people would experience internal states as diffuse, largely undifferentiated sensations.

If language provides inner states with a name and removes them from the realm of the unknown, social structure and social processes provide these states with a shape and a form. *Values*—widely held beliefs about what is important—and *norms*—guides to conduct—regulate which feelings may be experienced legitimately and how they may be expressed. People learn from others which activities (fist shaking or kissing) are associated with which feelings (rage or love), what identities they are expected to assume when these feelings are being expressed (angry son, willful spouse, devoted lover), and when, where, why, and how they may express them appropriately.

To summarize, self is an individual's consciousness of his or her own being and is achieved when a person is able to respond to himself or herself socially as an object, in the same fashion that he or she responds to other people as social objects. Self is a construct consisting of two dimensions: cognitive and affective. The "I" and the "me" represent phases (aspects) of the cognitive dimension of self. The affective dimension of self consists of feelings about the self—self-esteem or self-sentiment, which are defined shortly. The "I" phase of self (self as knower) is the *subjective* self, the "me" aspect of self (self as known) is the *objective* self.

Self-Concept

Despite her concern for analytical precision, Cass (1983/1984, 110) sidesteps the issue of defining self and offers instead this definition of self-concept: "the totality of the individual's thoughts and feelings having reference to himself as a social object."

Cass's definition of self-concept describes only one phase of self—the objective self—rather than self-concept as a whole. In addition, a rigorous analysis of the relation between self and self-concept requires a description of the components contained within the objective self and the relationships among the components.

As indicated earlier, objective self (the "me") consists of a cognitive dimension (thoughts about oneself) and an affective dimension (feelings about oneself). Atchley (1982, 390) separates the objective self into four components to enable more precise analysis: self-concept, ideal-self, self-evaluation, and self-esteem.

In the present analysis, *self-concept* refers to what people think they are like as individuals. Defined in this way, self-concept is synonymous with self-image, and is similar to the concept of identity as used traditionally by psychologists (e.g., Erikson 1959). *Ideal-self* refers to what people think they "ought to be like" as individuals. *Self-evaluation* refers to a moral appraisal of how well (or badly) people achieve their ideal-selves; and *self-esteem* refers to whether or not people like or dislike themselves, and to what degree.

Atchley (1982, 391) argues that self-concept and ideal-self are anchored in the positions people occupy in the social structure, the roles they play, and norms governing the expression and management of personal characteristics such as biological sex, social class, and gender. He adds that self-evaluation and self-esteem are similarly linked; they reflect "moral and emotional reactions" to the estimated fit between self-concept (what people think they are like) and ideal-self (what people think they ought to be like).

According to Atchley, self-evaluation and self-esteem are functions of the fit between self-concept and ideal-self. The closer the fit, the more positively the objective self will be evaluated and esteemed. Conversely, the greater the disparity between self-concept and ideal-self, the more negatively the objective self will be evaluated.

In summary, self-concept is one of four components that make up the dimension of objective self ("me"). The cognitive dimension of objective self consists of self-concept, ideal-self, and self-evaluation. The affective dimension of objective self contains the component of self-esteem.

Identity

As used here, *identity* is a cognitive construct referring to organized sets of characteristics that an individual perceives as representing the self definitively in relation to a social situation, imagined or real. My definition of identity is similar to the one developed by Gregory P. Stone (1962). Stone, however, focused on how identity is realized, while I emphasize what identity is conceptually.

Characteristics perceived as definitively representing the self assume the form of *attitudes* — potentials for action toward self or others — that are mobilized in relation to social situations. When removed from a given situation, the relevant identity becomes *dormant* or latent, part of a bundle of potentially relevant identities that make up a person's self-concept (Omark 1979, 1981b). The terms "social setting" and "social context" are synonymous with "social situations," as described below.

Identities perceived and experienced as relevant in many social situations are *transsituational* identities. The stigma surrounding homosexuality and the perceived need to keep homosexuality a secret may infuse homosexual identities with transsituational significance for many individuals at various times and places.

Cass (1983/1984) is inconsistent in describing the components of identity; initially she conceives of identity as having both cognitive and affective components:

> Identity refers to organized sets of self-perceptions [cognitions] and attached feelings [affects] that an individual holds about self with regard to some social category. (p. 110)

Later, however, she argues that "identity is a cognitive construct, 'classes of self-representations' "(p. 112).

Social Situations

Situations consist of all internal and external stimuli that act upon people during a given period. As strongly as physical dimensions, the symbolic dimensions of situations influence people's perceptions of, and responses to, internal and external stimuli.

People do not respond directly to stimuli, but to their *interpretations* of stimuli. They help one another interpret and define situations through communication. This is not to say that situations are created *de novo*. Most of the situations encountered routinely in social life are defined conventionally; that is, tradition has established fairly clear-cut norms governing conduct in common situations, which introduce stability to social interactions. Experience teaches people how they are expected to behave in certain everyday situations, such as classrooms, boardrooms, courthouses, churches or synagogues, and business conventions. Once they have assimilated situational norms, people know what is expected of them and of others in conventionally defined situations.

The ways in which situations are conventionally defined limit (but do not determine rigidly) the range of roles and identities that may be expressed legitimately (Stone and Farberman 1970b). Situations defined as religious, for example, encourage the adoption of "devout" identities and roles; the hushed and reverent tones that people adopt almost automatically when entering churches or synagogues express and announce "devout" roles and identities.

The characteristics seen as representing the self definitively in relation to social situations may be cognitive, affective, behavioral, or any of the three, such as the "parent" identity in the family setting or the "homosexual" identity in a same-sex lovemaking context. In addition, the identity characteristics themselves may vary in their perceived *value* (desirability), *salience* (prominence or visibility), *significance* (importance), *centrality* (essentiality), and *permanence* (fixedess).

The self-perceived value, salience, and significance of identity characteristics may also vary among situations and over time. Omark (1981b), for example, discusses at length how the perceived salience of homosexual identities varies among individuals and situations. A similar variability holds true for situationally mobilized identities — characteristics that people think represent them definitively in relation to a given setting. The individual may or may not perceive these self-identities as something one ought to be (implicating ideal-self); may or may not deem them morally correct (which involves self-evaluation); and may or may not enjoy them (which affects self-esteem). The maintenance of self-esteem may demand that either the perceived characteristic itself, the ideal-self, the self-concept, or all three be redefined to reduce the disparity between self-concept and ideal-self (Atchley 1982).

Identity and Self-Concept

Differences between self-concept and identity are revealed initially in the ways the concepts are defined. *Self-concept* refers to people's mental images of themselves — what they think they are like as people — and involves the issue of category membership. *Identity,* in contrast, refers to self-perceptions thought to represent the self definitively in specific social settings, such as the "doctor" identity at work and the "spouse" identity at home.

Self-concept is broader in scope than identity and encompasses a wider range of social categories; identity encompasses only situationally relevant dimensions of self-concept, social categories germane to the tasks at hand. Self-concept and identity differ in the sense that identity requires reference to a specific category in a social setting (imagined or real), whereas self-concept implicates a spectrum of social categories.

For Cass (1983/1984), the significant difference between self-concept and identity is point of reference:

> The components of self-concept (self-images) are the units upon which identity is built. The two constructs differ significantly in that identity necessitates reference to a specific social category while self-concept does not. (p. 111)

Cass believes that identity has a specific point of reference but that self-concept does not. Examination of the "social category" concept reveals the questionable nature of this assertion.

A *social category* is a "plurality of persons who are not organized into a system of social interaction but who do have similar social characteristics or statuses" (Theodorson and Theodorson 1969, 384). Examples of social categories are fathers, females, people over age fifty, redheads, and millionaires. Category membership may be achieved (millionaires), ascribed (redheads), or both achieved and ascribed (age). Members of such categories lack a sense of common awareness and shared identity; as a rule, they do not interact in an organized fashion or even necessarily know one another. Category members may or may not identify themselves as members.

Social categories and groups are important because of the cultural expectations and stereotypes surrounding them. Members are expected (correctly or not) to behave in certain ways, and to enact certain social roles. Potential members are exposed first to culturally based expectations about social categories (stereotypes) — outsiders' images of what category members are like as people — and may never learn the members' views of the category unless they gain an opportunity to interact with them (Goode 1981a; Omark 1978a). In some instances, members may not even know that they are members of a social category, as in the case of a severely retarded child, or that a social category exists to represent their interests, feelings, or behaviors, as in the case of "prehomosexual" children who grow up to lead homosexual lifestyles. I elaborate on this point in Chapter 4.

The interpretations and expectations that insiders place upon a social category may or may not differ considerably from those granted currency in the wider culture. Moreover, category members themselves differ in their interpretations of what category membership means and how it is to be expressed. When members of a social category identify with one another, share interests, and interact in a regular, organized fashion, they constitute a *group*.

Strauss (1969, 18-25) states that naming involves an act of placement in a category. Giving something a name *indicates* the object, that is, sets it apart from other objects, and *identifies* the object as such by placing it in a category. The definitive characteristics of the object provide the basis for classification and evaluation.

It is not useful or accurate to claim that self-concept differs from identity in that self-concept lacks reference to a social category. Both self-concept and identity involve naming or category placement. Thoughts about what one is like as a person (self-concept) are expressed in categorical terms and provide the basis for identity in various settings. The statement "I am female, old, liberal, and upwardly mobile," for example, is a conception of self that contains references to the social categories of sex, age, political orientation, and social class. Each or any of these social categories may provide foundations for identity in many social settings.

The definition of identity offered here is logically consistent with the framework developed in this chapter for discussing self and identity. Self-concept is viewed as part of the cognitive dimension of objective self. Identity is classified as a cognitive construct, a subset of self-concept, mobilized in social contexts where it is pertinent. Both self-concept and identity involve named characteristics. Naming involves placing a characteristic or an attribute into a category; as part of self-concept, named characteristics or attributes are evaluated according to how they relate to ideal-self. The closer the fit between a characteristic and the ideal-self, the more highly the characteristic will be esteemed; in turn, the degree of esteem implicates the affective dimension of the objective self.

Self-concept and identity differ in that identity requires reference to social categories relevant to a specific social setting or situation, whereas self-concept implicates a wider range of social categories. Hence identity refers to the labels that an individual sees as representing the self definitively in a social situation. When the person is removed from the situation, the identity becomes latent (Omark 1981b). In short, a person has one self-concept and many situationally relevant identities. The term *self-identity* is synonymous with identity as defined above.

Homosexual Identity

Homosexual identity is classified here as a cognitive construct and a component of self-concept. As formally defined here, *homosexual identity* refers to a perception of self as homosexual in relation to social settings, imagined or real, defined as romantic or sexual. A perception of self as homosexual assumes the form of an *attitude*—a potential line of action regarding self or others—that is mobilized in romantic or sexual settings.

Self-placement in the social category "homosexual" is a necessary part of homosexual identity formation. As Chapter 4 makes clear, "coming out" to oneself is a major event in the process of homosexual identity formation and refers to the decision "to define oneself [to oneself] as homosexual" (Dank 1971, 181). Self-placement in the social category "homosexual" occurs commonly through interactions with other self-defined homosexuals (Dank 1971; Harry and DeVall 1978; Plummer 1975; Ponse 1978; Troiden 1977, 1979; Warren 1974; Weinberg 1978).

Like other identities, the homosexual identity is one of several identities incorporated into a person's self-concept. In addition, it exists at three analytically separable levels. Depending on context, it may function as a self-identity, a perceived identity, a presented identity, or all three (Cass 1983/1984).

The homosexual identity is a *self-identity* when an individual sees himself or herself as homosexual in relation to romantic or sexual settings. The term "self-identity" is synonymous with the term "identity," as defined above. It is a *perceived identity* in situations when the individual thinks or knows that others view him or her as homosexual. It is a *presented identity* when an individual presents or announces herself or himself as homosexual in concrete social settings.

Homosexual identities are most fully *realized*—brought into concrete existence—when self-identity, perceived identity, and presented identity coincide; that is, where an accord exists among who people think they are, who they claim they are, and how others view them. Cass's (1983/1984) uses of these distinctions are similar to my own, but the bases are different. I link the concept of identity with social categories and social settings, whereas she associates identity with social categories.

Uses of the Term Homosexual

The term *homosexual* may have two different meanings in general usage. As a noun, *homosexual* classifies the objective self as a specific "type" on the basis of what is perceived as an essential condition or form of being. Homosexuals themselves use the term in this fashion (Faderman 1984/1985; Ponse 1978, 1980; Warren 1974, 1980). As an adjective, *homosexual* describes behavior, fantasies, or desires involving the same sex; these are ways of acting, thinking, or feeling rather than states or qualities of being (Plummer 1981a).

A fundamental principle of sociology is that people often identify themselves in terms of the roles they play. Self-identifications anchored in behavior, feelings, or fantasies thought to reflect essential needs are perceived as especially meaningful. For this reason, this book adopts an "insider's" perspective on the term *homosexual*—that is, uses it as a noun to denote self-placement in the "homosexual" social category.

People also place themselves in a social position or status when they label themselves as homosexual. The homosexual role is the pattern of behavior associated with the status of "homosexual," which is socially disvalued in the United States. People typically learn first about the homosexual role from outsiders, from the perspective of the wider, stigmatizing society. Later, if at all, they learn about the role from insiders, from the point of view of homosexuals themselves (Goode 1981a, 1981b).

The insider's perspective toward homosexuality is by no means uniform. A variety of identities and roles are available to members of the homosexual community; the form and content of the homosexual role vary within and among cultures (Plummer 1984). In fact, Humphreys and Miller (1980, 144-49) argue that the "homosexual subculture" has become sufficiently complex and diverse to warrant the label "homosexual satellite culture." The diverse identities and roles available to lesbians and gay males are described at length in Chapter 5.

Contact with members of the homosexual satellite culture plays a crucial role in homosexual identity formation. Initial encounters with other self-defined homosexuals provide the neophyte with a series of "accounts" (Scott and Lyman 1968) or "vocabularies of motives" (Mills 1940) that "excuse," "justify," and "legitimize" homosexual feelings and behavior. Accounts neutralize the negative images that people have absorbed from the wider society in the process of socialization and transform the meaning of the cognitive category "homosexual" from something bad to something good. Homosexuality is redefined in terms more positive for the self. Evidence suggests that subculturally involved homosexuals exhibit higher levels of self-esteem than those involved only marginally in the subculture

(Bell and Weinberg 1978; Harry and DeVall 1978; Ross 1978; Weinberg and Williams 1974).

The issue of self-esteem and homosexuality has subtle, yet profound, sociopolitical implications. No significant differences have been noted between levels of self-esteem in lesbians and gay males and in heterosexual controls, and Adam (1978b) believes that this finding undermines the argument that homosexuals possess "pathological personalities." Conversely, the finding of "no difference" justifies and maintains the political status quo.

> Parallel to the hidden dialogue in studies of black self-esteem, the obliteration of difference once again absolves the larger society of any need to evaluate persecutory practices or opportunity structures. An oppressive social structure has thereby been absolved of responsibility in the problems experienced by gay people. (Adam 1978b, 50)

Theoretical Implications

In American society, the aim and direction of sexual desire is viewed as a relatively fixed, stable, and essential aspect of personality (Richardson 1981a, 1983/1984). Thus the centrality and significance that many homosexuals attribute to their homosexual identities reflects in part beliefs given widespread currency in the wider society. Many homosexuals attribute a transsituational significance to their identities; they see them as relevant to most interactions and situations.

Researchers have identified a number of factors that infuse homosexual identities with transsituational significance: the social stigma surrounding homosexuality and homosexuals (Cass 1979; Plummer 1975; Ponse 1978, 1980; Troiden 1977, 1979; Warren 1974, 1980); the lack of legitimacy accorded bisexual options (Blumstein and Schwartz 1974, 1977; Humphreys 1979; Paul 1985; Warren 1974); the culturally defined link between homosexuality and gender-inappropriate behaviors (Cass 1979; Harry 1982; Hart and Richardson 1981; Plummer 1975, 1981b; Troiden 1977); the "heterosexual assumption" — the presumption that everyone is heterosexual and that the logical progression of adult life includes marriage and family (Plummer 1981a; Ponse 1978); and the tendency of dominant groups to "inferiorize" minorities to protect the "hierarchy of access" (Adam 1978a).

For these reasons, many homosexuals view their homosexual identities as defining characteristics of self at some points in their lives, and as attributes relevant to most social interactions and situations. In their eyes, the homosexual attribute dwarfs all others; it becomes a *master status* (Becker

1963). Whether they perceive their homosexual identities consistently as central and significant throughout their lives, however, remains an empirical question.

Chapter 4

A MODEL OF HOMOSEXUAL
IDENTITY FORMATION

This chapter develops an ideal-typical model that describes how committed homosexuals—men and women who have defined themselves as homosexual and adopted homosexuality as a way of life—recall their arrival at perceptions of self as homosexual in relation to romantic and sexual settings. More specifically, the chapter describes ideal types, reviews models for homosexual identity formation that influenced the present work, presents a four-stage ideal-typical model of homosexual identity formation in both lesbians and gay males, and calls attention to the variables that influence rates of homosexual identity formation.

Ideal Types

Ideal types represent abstractions based on concrete observations of the phenomena under investigation. They are heuristic devices—ways of organizing materials for analytical and comparative purposes. These types are not real; nothing and nobody fits them exactly (Theodorson and Theodorson 1969).

Ideal types are used as benchmarks against which to describe, compare, and test hypotheses relating to empirical reality (Theodorson and Theodorson, 1969); they are frameworks for ordering observations logically. Ideal types are similar to stereotypes except that they are examined and refined continuously to correspond more closely to the empirical reality that they try to represent. At best, ideal models capture general patterns encountered by many individuals; variations are expected and explained, and often lead to revisions of ideal types.

The four-stage model of homosexual identity formation outlined here describes only general patterns encountered by committed homosexuals —women and men who see themselves as homosexual and adopt corresponding lifestyles. Often-repeated themes in the life histories of lesbians and gay males, clustered according to life stages, provide the content and characteristics of each stage. Progress through the various stages increases the probability of homosexual identity formation, but does not determine it fully. A shifting effect is involved; some men and women "drift away" at various points before the fourth and final stage and never adopt homosexual identities or lead homosexual lifestyles.

Themes of Models

During the past decade, several investigators have proposed theoretical models that attempt to explain the formation of homosexual identities (Cass 1979, 1984; Coleman 1982; Lee 1977; Minton and McDonald 1983/1984; Plummer 1975; Ponse 1978; Schäfer 1976; Sophie 1985/1986; Troiden 1977, 1979; Weinberg 1977, 1978). Although the various models suggest different numbers of stages to explain homosexual identity formation, they describe strikingly similar patterns of growth and change as major hallmarks of homosexual identity formation.

First, nearly all the models view homosexual identity formation as taking place against a backdrop of stigma. The stigma surrounding homosexuality affects both the formation and management of homosexual identities. Second, homosexual identities are described as developing over a protracted period and involving a number of "growth points or changes" that may be ordered into a series of stages (Cass 1984). Third, homosexual identity formation involves increasing acceptance of the label "homosexual" as applied to the self. Fourth, although "coming out" begins when individuals define themselves to themselves as homosexual, lesbians and gay males typically report an increased desire over time to disclose their homosexual identity to at least some members of an expanding series of audiences. Thus, coming out, or identity disclosure, takes place at a number of levels: to self, to other homosexuals, to heterosexual friends and family, to co-workers, and to the public at large (Coleman 1982; Lee 1977). Finally, lesbians and gays develop "increasingly personalized and frequent" social contacts with other homosexuals over time (Cass 1984).

Major Works

The four-stage model developed later in this chapter is a revision of my earlier work, which synthesized and elaborated on Plummer's (1975) model of "becoming homosexual." The revised model incorporates insights provided by Barbara Ponse's (1978) and Vivienne Cass's (1979, 1984) theorizing and research on homosexual identity formation. Because the works of Plummer, my earlier research, and the investigations by Ponse and Cass influenced my revised model of homosexual identity formation, I discuss each prototype briefly.

Plummer

According to Plummer (1975), homosexual identity formation is part of the larger process of "becoming homosexual," that is, adopting homosexuality as a way of life. Becoming homosexual involves the decision to define oneself as homosexual, the learning of homosexual roles, and the decision to live one's adult life as a practicing homosexual. Plummer believes that males who adopt homosexuality as a way of life pass through a "career" consisting of four stages.

In the *sensitization* stage, boys gain childhood experiences that may later serve as bases for defining themselves as homosexual. These experiences are gained in three areas: *social* (gender-inappropriate interests), *emotional* (same-sex emotional attachments), and *genital* (same-sex genital activities). Childhood experiences sensitize boys to interpret past events as indicating a homosexual potential.

Signification and disorientation occur during adolescence. During this stage, boys begin to speculate that their interests and feelings "might" be homosexual. Their awareness of homosexuality and its potential relevance to self is subsequently heightened (signified). The homosexual implications of their activities, feelings, or interests produces anxiety and confusion (disorientation).

Boys establish contact with other homosexuals, self-define as homosexual, and begin to learn homosexual roles during the *coming-out* stage, which typically begins at some point during middle to late adolescence. Finally, *stabilization* occurs when they become comfortable with homosexuality and committed to it as a way of life.

Further research and theorizing on homosexual identity formation has revealed some problems with Plummer's theoretical account. First, his analysis focuses on men who adopt homosexuality as a way of life, but neglects homosexual identity formation in lesbians. Second, he does not define homosexual identity or indicate its relationship to self-concept. Third, his account is theoretical rather than empirical; he did not test his model against the experiences of a sample of gay males.

Troiden

My own research (Troiden 1977, 1979) on acquisition of gay identity, using a sample of 150 homosexual men, provides empirical support for a theoretical framework similar to Plummer's. This formulation also consists of four stages: sensitization, dissociation and signification, coming out, and commitment.

The sensitization and coming-out stages are comparable to those described by Plummer, but *dissociation* consists of the conscious partitioning of sexual feelings or activity from sexual identity. Rather than diminish the awareness of possible homosexual feelings, dissociation has the unintended and ironic effect of signifying or highlighting the feelings. Finally, *commitment* presupposes a reluctance to abandon the homosexual identity even in the face of an opportunity to do so. Happiness and satisfaction with the homosexual identity and lifestyle also characterize the commitment stage.

This model also has its shortcomings. It focuses only on males, fails to give a clear definition of homosexual identity, and neglects to distinguish between, and relate, the concepts of self-concept and identity (Cass 1983/1984).

Ponse

Barbara Ponse's (1978) sociological study of identities in the lesbian world focused on how lesbian identities are formed in relation to the norms of the lesbian community. She contacted informants in her observational study through self-help organizations of overt homosexual women and friendship networks among covert lesbians. Seventy-five informants took part, thirty- six of whom were interviewed in depth (Ponse 1984).

Ponse's research identified a "gay trajectory" consisting of five elements that serve as possible steps toward assuming lesbian identities. The first element is a subjective sense of difference from heterosexuals, which is identified as an emotional or sexual preference for other women. Next, women gain an understanding of the lesbian or homosexual significance of their sexual or romantic feelings. The third element is the assumption of a lesbian identity. Fourth, these women seek the company of similarly situated women. Fifth and last, they become involved in lesbian emotional or sexual relationships.

The first three steps are of primary importance from the perspective of the lesbian community. Given these three elements, "the individual will experience a sense of strain toward the other two" (Ponse 1978, 125). Ponse found wide variations in the order in which her informants encountered elements of the gay trajectory. I shall return to this point.

Ponse's study led her to conclude that it is difficult to define who "really is" lesbian; a certain amount of independence exists between identity and activity. She identified four combinations of identity and activity and determined that women can and do shift from one to another: lesbian identity and lesbian activity; lesbian identity without lesbian activity (e.g., celibacy or heterosexual activity); lesbian activity without lesbian identity (e.g., heterosexual or bisexual identity); and heterosexual activity and heterosexual identity. Similar distinctions have been drawn for gay males (Troiden 1977; Warren 1974) as well as for lesbians (Blumstein and Schwartz 1974).

A majority of the women interviewed by Ponse fell into the category of lesbian identity and activity, and saw the lesbian identity as "an emanation from the essential self: lesbianism is a totality of which sexuality is a mere part" (Ponse 1978, 171). The gay males observed by Carol Warren (1974) drew a similar distinction between "being" gay and "doing" homosexual activity.

Ponse also distinguishes between *primary* lesbians, *elective* lesbians, and women with *idiosyncratic* identities. For primary lesbians, memories of sexual or emotional attractions to the same sex predated puberty, and few of these women reported heterosexual experiences. Elective lesbians, in contrast, generally identified their feelings as homosexual at much later ages, and most reported heterosexual experiences. Bell, Weinberg, and Hammersmith (1981a, 201) make the same point when they distinguish between exclusive homosexuals and bisexuals. Finally, women with idiosyncratic identities generally viewed themselves as heterosexual or bisexual, even though they were involved in meaningful lesbian relationships or participating actively in the lesbian subculture.

Ponse's analysis of lesbian identity suffers a few limitations. First, her work details the range of identities and roles available to women in the lesbian community instead of describing how women came to assume their lesbian identities in the first place. Second, although the women in her sample encountered the elements making up the gay trajectory in somewhat different orders, some of this variation may be explained by her small sample size and the fact that her analysis includes all four combinations of identity and activity described above. Third, she did not ask her informants standardized questions to determine, for example, the age at which they recalled first becoming aroused by the same sex, or the age of first homosexual activity. Thus she had no way of determining the modal pattern for her informants. Fourth, had she focused only on women with lesbian identities and activities, as in the present study, she might have found less variation along the gay trajectory.

Cass

Vivienne Cass's (1979) theoretical account of homosexual identity formation was the first attempt at explaining homosexual identity development in both lesbians and gay males. Her original formulation cast homosexual identity development into a mold involving six stages.

Before stage 1, according to Cass, people believe they are heterosexual and never question this assumption. During the first stage, *identity confusion,* they begin to think they might possibly be homosexual. In the second stage, *identity comparison,* people begin to believe they are probably homosexual. Women and men define themselves as homosexual during the *identity tolerance* stage, but remain uncomfortable with their homosexual identities. "Contacting other homosexuals is viewed as 'something that *has* to be done' in order to counter the felt isolation and alienation from others" (Cass 1979, 229; italics added). The fourth stage, *identity acceptance,* occurs in the wake of positive contacts with other lesbians and gays who provide neophytes with information and justifications that "normalize" homosexuality as an identity and a lifestyle.

During the fifth stage, *identity pride,* gays and lesbians are proud to be homosexual and enjoy their homosexual lifestyles. They do not hide their homosexuality, but frequently disclose it to others. Moreover, they become angry when exposed to the antihomosexual attitudes held by many heterosexuals, and vigorously defend homosexuality in their presence. For this reason, lesbians and gay males prefer to mix socially with other homosexuals during this stage.

During *identity synthesis,* gay males and lesbians are prepared to tell anyone they are homosexual, although they no longer perceive their homosexual identities as the most important part of themselves. Although occasionally angered by antihomosexual sentiments, they have learned through experience that many heterosexuals accept homosexuals comfortably. In this final stage, gay males and lesbians mix socially with both homosexuals and heterosexuals.

Cass (1984) tested her theoretical model with a specially developed questionnaire. Analysis of results obtained from 103 gay males and sixty-three lesbians revealed no clear-cut boundaries between stages 1 and 2 (identity confusion, identity comparison) and stages 5 and 6 (identity pride, identity synthesis); the hypothesized differences between these stages are indistinct. Cass concluded that homosexual identities may be formed in four stages: identity confusion, identity tolerance, identity acceptance, and identity synthesis.

Although Cass's (1979, 1983/1984, 1984) scholarship on homosexual identity formation is theoretically and empirically rigorous, critical evaluation of her work reveals some shortcomings. First, her model ignores the role of childhood genital, emotional, and social experiences in creating alienation and perceptions of difference that contribute to initial feelings of identity confusion. Second, her conceptualization of homosexual identity equates identity *development* with identity *disclosure.* For Cass, a homosexual identity is "fully evolved" only when individuals disclose the identity to "*all* others constituting the individual's social environment"

(1983/1984, 111). An identity option—degree of openness about the homosexual identity—becomes a prerequisite for full identity development. Because most homosexuals do not disclose their identities to most people (as is demonstrated later in this chapter), Cass's model would characterize them as "developmentally arrested."

Identity disclosure is more a matter of identity management than identity development. Strictly speaking, homosexual identities are developed when individuals define themselves as such, but a shift of emphasis does occur in the wake of homosexual self-labeling. Questions about sexual identity are replaced by concerns about managing the stigma attached to homosexual identities and lifestyles.

Identity disclosure, however, is an overt indication of commitment to homosexuality as a way of life. To the extent that people routinely present themselves as homosexual in most or all social settings, their homosexual identities are realized—brought into concrete existence—more frequently than those of people who disclose their identities less frequently, if at all.

Third, when Cass asserts that the homosexual identity (a cognition) is not developed fully without full self-disclosure in all settings (a behavior), she mixes cognitive and behavioral elements within the same construct, something she claims must be avoided for the sake of conceptual clarity.

Fourth, although Cass conceptualizes identity tolerance and identity acceptance as two different stages, identity tolerance may be viewed as the beginning, and identity acceptance as the end, of a single stage. During this stage, people define themselves as homosexual, begin to associate with other homosexuals, learn homosexual roles, and acquire a series of "accounts" (Scott and Lyman 1968) or "vocabularies of motives" (Mills 1940) that excuse, justify, or legitimize homosexual feelings and behavior. In this way, they neutralize the negative views of homosexuals absorbed from the wider, stigmatizing society.

An Ideal-Typical Model

Sensitization, the first stage in my four-stage model, is borrowed from Plummer. Stage 2, identity confusion, combines insights borrowed from Plummer, Cass, and my earlier model. The third stage, identity assumption, incorporates Cass's hypothesized stages of identity tolerance and acceptance and the "coming out" stage from my earlier model. The fourth stage, commitment, builds on my earlier model; it posits identity disclosure (from Cass) as an identity option rather than a separate stage, and as an external indicator of commitment to homosexuality as a way of life. Theoretical insights borrowed from Ponse are incorporated throughout the model.

Sociological analysis of homosexual identity formation begins with an examination of the social contexts and patterns of interaction that lead individuals to accumulate a series of sexual meanings, which predispose them to identify themselves subsequently as homosexual (Plummer 1975). The meanings of feelings or activities, sexual or otherwise, are not self-evident. Before people can identify themselves in terms of a social condition or category, they must learn that a social category representing the activity or feelings exists (e.g., homosexual preferences or behavior); learn that other people occupy the social category (e.g., that homosexuals exist as a group); learn that their own socially constructed needs and interests are more similar to those who occupy the social category than they are different; begin to identify with those included in the social category; decide that they qualify for membership in the social category on the basis of activity and feelings in various settings; elect to label themselves in terms of the social category, that is, define themselves as "being" the social category in contexts where category membership is relevant; and incorporate and absorb these situationally linked identities into their self-concepts over time (Lofland 1969; McCall and Simmons 1966; Simmons 1965).

A word of warning: From an interactionist perspective, although identities develop over time in a series of stages, identity formation is not conceptualized as a linear, step-by-step process, in which one stage follows and builds on another, with fluctuations written off as regressions. Instead, the process of homosexual identity formation resembles a horizontal spiral, like a spring lying on its side. Progress through the stages occurs in a back-and-forth, up-and-down fashion; the stages overlap and recur in somewhat different ways for different people (McWhirter and Mattison 1984). In many instances, stages are encountered in consecutive order, but sometimes they are merged, glossed over, bypassed, or realized simultaneously. In particular, the approximate ages outlined for each stage are rough guidelines. Because these ages are based on averages, variations are to be expected and should not be treated as regressions. People also vary somewhat in the order in which they encounter homosexual events (e.g., age at first homosexual activity).

Stage 1: Sensitization

The *sensitization* stage occurs before puberty. At this time, most lesbians and gay males do not see homosexuality as personally relevant; that is, they assume they are heterosexual, if they think about their sexual status at all. Lesbians and gay males, however, typically acquire social experiences during their childhoods that serve later as bases for seeing homosexuality as personally relevant, lending support to emerging perceptions of themselves as possibly homosexual. In short, childhood experiences sensitize lesbians and gays to subsequent self-definition as homosexual. Sensitization parallels Minton and McDonald's (1983/1984) "egocentric" stage.

Sensitization is characterized by generalized feelings of marginality, perceptions of being different from same-sex peers. The following comments illustrate the forms these childhood feelings of difference assumed for lesbians: "I wasn't interested in boys"; "I was more interested in the arts and in intellectual things"; "I was very shy and unaggressive"; "I felt different: unfeminine, ungraceful, not very pretty, kind of a mess"; "I was becoming aware of my homosexuality. It's a staggering thing for a kid that age to live with"; "I was more masculine, more independent, more aggressive, more outdoorish"; "I didn't express myself the way other girls would. For example, I never showed my feelings. I wasn't emotional" (Bell, Weinberg, and Hammersmith 1981a, 148, 156).

Similar themes of childhood marginality are echoed in the comments of gay males: "I had a keener interest in the arts"; "I couldn't stand sports, so naturally that made me different. A ball thrown at me was like a bomb"; "I never learned to fight"; "I wasn't interested in laying girls in the cornfields. It turned me off completely"; "I just didn't feel I was like other boys. I was very fond of pretty things like ribbons and flowers and music"; "I began to get feelings I was gay. I'd notice other boys' bodies in the gym and masturbate excessively"; "I was indifferent to boys' games, like cops and robbers. I was more interested in watching insects and reflecting on certain things"; and "I was called the sissy of the family. I had been very pointedly told that I was effeminate" (Bell, Weinberg, and Hammersmith 1981a, 74, 86).

Research by Bell, Weinberg, and Hammersmith (1981a) found that homosexual males ($N = 573$) were almost twice as likely (72% vs. 39%) as heterosexual controls ($N = 284$) to report feeling "very much or somewhat" different from other boys during grade school (grades 1-8). Lesbians ($N = 229$) were also more likely than heterosexual controls ($N = 101$) to have felt "somewhat or very much" different from other girls during grade school (72% vs. 54%).

During sensitization, childhood social experiences play a larger role than emotional or genital events in generating perceptions of difference. Both lesbians and gay males in the Bell, Weinberg, and Hammersmith sample saw gender-neutral or gender-inappropriate interests or behaviors as generating their feelings of marginality (the social realm). Only a minority of the lesbians and gay males felt different because of same-sex attractions (the emotional realm) or sexual activities (the genital realm).

More specifically, lesbians in the Bell, Weinberg, and Hammersmith study were more likely than heterosexual controls to say they felt different because they were more "masculine" than other girls (34% vs. 9%), because they were more interested in sports (20% vs. 2%), or because they had homosexual interests or lacked heterosexual interests (15% vs. 2%). Moreover, fewer lesbians than heterosexual controls (13% vs. 55%) reported having enjoyed typical girls' activities (e.g., hopscotch, jacks, playing house), but lesbians were much more likely (71% vs. 28%) to say they enjoyed typical boys' activities (e.g., baseball, football).

In a similar vein, homosexual males were more likely than heterosexual controls to report that they felt odd because they did not like sports (48% vs. 21%), because they were "feminine" (23% vs. 1%), or because they were not sexually interested in girls or were sexually interested in other boys (18% vs. 1%). Gay males were also significantly more likely than heterosexual controls (68% vs. 34%) to report having enjoyed solitary activities associated only indirectly with gender (e.g., reading, drawing, music). Moreover, homosexual males were much less likely than heterosexual controls (11% vs. 70%) to report having enjoyed boys' activities (e.g., football, baseball) "very much" during childhood.

Although a sense of being different and set apart from same-sex age mates is a persistent theme in the childhood experiences of lesbians and gay males, research indicates that only a minority of gay males (20%) and lesbians (20%) begin to see themselves as *sexually* different before age twelve, and fewer still—only 4 percent of the females and 4 percent of the males—label this difference as "homosexual" while they are children (Bell, Weinberg, and Hammersmith 1981b, 82-83). It is not surprising that "prehomosexuals" used gender metaphors rather than sexual metaphors to interpret and explain their childhood feelings of difference; the mastery of gender roles rather than sexual scripts is emphasized during childhood (Doyle 1983; Tavris and Wade 1984). Although they may have engaged in heterosexual and/or homosexual sex play, children do not appear to define their sexual experimentation in heterosexual or homosexual terms. The socially created categories of homosexual, heterosexual, and bisexual hold little or no significance for them. Physical acts become meaningful only when they are embedded in sexual scripts, which are acquired during adolescence (Gagnon and Simon 1973). For these reasons, prehomosexuals rarely wonder, "Am I a homosexual?" or believe that homosexuality has anything to do with them personally while they are children.

The significance of sensitization resides in the meanings attached *subsequently* to childhood experiences, rather than the experiences themselves. Because sociocultural arrangements in American society articulate linkages between gender-inappropriate behavior and homosexuality, gender-neutral or gender-atypical activities and interests during childhood provide many women and men with a potential basis for subsequent interpretations of self as possibly homosexual. Childhood experiences gained in social, emotional, and genital realms come to be invested with homosexual significance during adolescence. The reinterpretation of past events as indicating a homosexual potential appears to be a necessary (but not sufficient) condition for the eventual adoption of homosexual identities.

Stage 2: Identity Confusion

Lesbians and gay males typically begin to personalize homosexuality during adolescence, when they begin to reflect upon the idea that their feelings or behaviors could be regarded as homosexual. The thought that they are potentially homosexual is dissonant with previously held self-images. The hallmark of this stage is *identity confusion* — inner turmoil and uncertainty surrounding their ambiguous sexual status. The sexual identities of lesbians and gay males are in limbo; they can no longer take their heterosexual identities as given, but they have yet to develop perceptions of themselves as homosexual. Minton and McDonald (1983/1984) draw a similar portrait in their "sociocentric" stage, and Sophie (1985/1986) calls this the "first awareness" stage of lesbian identity formation.

Cass (1984) describes the early phase of identity confusion in the following way:

> You are not sure who you are. You are confused about what sort of person you are and where your life is going. You ask yourself the questions "Who am I?," "Am I a homosexual?," "Am I really a heterosexual?" (p. 156)

By middle or late adolescence, a perception of self as "probably" homosexual begins to emerge. In retrospective studies involving adults, gay males begin to suspect that they "might" be homosexual at an average age of seventeen (Troiden 1979; Troiden and Goode 1980), lesbians at an average age of eighteen (Schäfer 1976).

Cass (1984) describes the later phase of identity confusion as follows:

> You feel that you *probably* are a homosexual, although you're not definitely sure. You feel distant or cut off from [other people]. You are beginning to think that it might help to meet other homosexuals but you're not sure whether you really want to or not. You prefer to put on a front of being completely heterosexual. (p. 156)

Several factors are responsible for the identity confusion experienced during this phase: altered perceptions of self, the experience of heterosexual and homosexual arousal and behavior, the stigma attached to homosexuality, and inaccurate knowledge about homosexuals and homosexuality.

Altered perceptions of self are partly responsible for the identity confusion experienced during this phase. Childhood perceptions of self as different crystallize into perceptions of self as sexually different after the onset of adolescence. Whereas only 20 percent of the lesbians and gay males in the Bell, Weinberg, and Hammersmith (1981a) study saw themselves as sexually different before age twelve, 74 percent of the lesbians and 84 percent of the gay males felt sexually different by age nineteen, as compared to only 10 percent of the heterosexual female and 11 percent of the heterosexual male controls. For both homosexual women and men, the most frequently cited reasons for feeling sexually different were homosexual interests and/or the lack of heterosexual interests. Gender atypicality was mentioned, but not as frequently. Thus genital and emotional experiences, more than social experiences, seem to precipitate perceptions of self as sexually different during the stage of identity confusion.

Another source of identity confusion is found in sexual experience itself. Recent investigations of homosexuality have revealed consistently that homosexuals exhibit greater variability in their childhood and adolescent sexual feelings and behaviors than heterosexuals (Bell and Weinberg 1978; Bell, Weinberg, and Hammersmith 1981b; Saghir and Robins 1973; Schäfer 1976; Weinberg and Williams 1974). By early to middle adolescence, most lesbians and gay males have experienced both heterosexual and homosexual arousal and behavior. Only a minority of the Bell, Weinberg, and Hammersmith sample, for example — 28 percent of the gay males and 21 percent of lesbians — were *never* sexually aroused by the opposite sex, and only 21 percent of the males and 12 percent of the females reported never having an opposite-sex encounter that they or others considered sexual. Thus significant majorities of lesbians and gay males experience heterosexual and homosexual arousal and behavior before age nineteen. Since American society portrays people as either homosexual or heterosexual, it is not surprising that adolescent lesbians and gay males are uncertain and confused regarding their sexual orientations.

As a general rule, gay males are aware of their same-sex attractions at earlier ages than lesbians. Males report awareness of their same-sex feelings at an average age of thirteen (Bell, Weinberg, and Hammersmith 1981a; Dank 1971; Kooden et al. 1979; McDonald 1982). The corresponding average age for lesbians is between fourteen and sixteen (Bell, Weinberg, and Hammersmith 1981a; Riddle and Morin 1977). Gay males first act on their sexual feelings at an average age of fifteen (Bell, Weinberg, and Hammersmith 1981a; Kooden et al. 1979; McDonald 1982; Troiden 1979; Troiden and Goode 1980), whereas lesbians first act on their sexual feelings at an average age of twenty, four to six years after first awareness of their same-sex attractions (Bell, Weinberg, and Hammersmith 1981a; Riddle and Morin 1977; Schäfer 1976).

The stigma surrounding homosexuality also contributes to identity confusion because it discourages adolescent (and some adult) lesbians and gay males from discussing their emerging sexual desires and/or activities with either age mates or families. As Plummer (1975) has noted, the societal condemnation of homosexuality creates problems of guilt, secrecy, and difficulty in gaining access to other homosexuals. Moreover, the emphasis placed on gender roles and the privatization of sexuality compounds identity confusion and aloneness.

Ignorance and inaccurate knowledge about homosexuality also contribute to identity confusion. People are unlikely to identify themselves in terms of a social category as long as they are unaware that the category exists, lack accurate information about the kinds of people who occupy the category, or believe they have nothing in common with category members (Lofland 1969). In other words, before they can see themselves as homosexual, people must realize that homosexuality and homosexuals exist, learn what homosexuals are actually like as people, and be able to perceive similarities between their own desires and behaviors and those of people labeled socially as homosexual. Today, accurate information about homosexuality has been circulated and distributed throughout society, making it easier to identify homosexual elements in feelings and activities (Dank 1971; Troiden 1979; Troiden and Goode 1980). Lesbians and gay males first understand what the term homosexual means at approximately the same time, at the average age of sixteen or seventeen respectively (Riddle and Morin 1977). Knowledge about the term homosexual may be acquired more rapidly in urban areas than in rural areas, where homosexuality is less likely to be discussed.

Lesbians and gay males typically respond to identity confusion by adopting one or more of the following strategies: denial (Goode 1984; Troiden 1977); repair (Humphreys 1972) avoidance (Cass 1979); redefinition (Cass 1979; Troiden 1977); and acceptance (Cass 1979; Troiden 1977).

Gay males and lesbians who use *denial* disclaim the homosexual component to their feelings, fantasies, or activities. *Repair* involves wholesale attempts to eradicate homosexual feelings and behaviors. Professional help is sought to eliminate the sexual feelings, fantasies, or activities considered unacceptable.

Avoidance is a third overall strategy for dealing with identity confusion (Cass 1979). Although avoidant women and men recognize that their behavior, thoughts, or fantasies are homosexual, they regard them as unacceptable, something to be avoided.

Avoidance may assume at least one of several forms. Some teenaged (and adult) men and women *inhibit* the behaviors or interests they have learned to associate with homosexuality: "I thought my sexual interest in other girls would go away if I paid more attention to boys and concentrated more on being feminine"; "I figured I'd go straight and develop more of an interest in girls if I got even more involved in sports and didn't spend as much time on my art" (author's files).

Some adolescent men and women *limit* their *opposite-sex exposure* to prevent peers or family from learning about their relative lack of heterosexual responsiveness: "I hated dating. I was always afraid I wouldn't get erect when we petted and made out and that the girls would find out I was probably gay." "I felt really weird compared to the other girls. I couldn't understand why they thought guys were so great. I dated only to keep my parents off my back" (author's files).

Other gay males and lesbians *limit* their *exposure to information* about homosexuality during adolescence because they fear that the information may confirm their suspected homosexuality: "Your first lecture on homosexuality awakened my fears of being homosexual. I cut class during the homosexuality section and skipped the assigned readings. I just couldn't accept the idea of being a lesbian" (author's files); "One ingenious defense was to remain as ignorant as possible on the subject of homosexuality. No one would ever catch *me* at the 'Ho' drawer of the New York Public Library Card Catalog" (Reid 1973, 40).

Another avoidance strategy is to assume *antihomosexual postures*. Some teenaged (and adult) men and women distance themselves from their own homoerotic feelings by attacking and ridiculing homosexuals: "At one time I hated myself because of sexual feelings for men. I'm ashamed to admit that I made a nellie guy's life miserable because of it"; "I really put down masculine acting women until I came out and realized that not all lesbians act that way and that many straight women do" (author's files).

Heterosexual immersion is another strategy for avoidance. Some adolescent lesbians and gay males establish heterosexual involvements at varying levels of intimacy in order to eliminate their "inappropriate" sexual interests: "I thought my homosexual feelings would go away if I dated a lot and had sex with as many women as possible"; "I thought my attraction to women was a passing phase and would go away once I started having intercourse with my boyfriend" (author's files). In some instances, an adolescent girl may purposely become pregnant as a means of "proving" that she could not possibly be homosexual.

Another avoidance strategy is *escapism*. Some adolescent lesbians and gay males avoid confronting their homosexual erotic feelings through the use and abuse of chemical substances. Getting high on drugs provides temporary relief from feelings of identity confusion and may be used to justify sexual feelings and behaviors ordinarily viewed as unacceptable.

A fourth general means of reducing identity confusion is to *redefine* behavior, feelings, or context along more conventional lines. (Plummer

[1984] calls redefinition "neutralization.") Redefinition is reflected in the use of special-case, ambisexual, temporary-identity (Cass 1979), or situational strategies.

In the *special-case* strategy, homosexual behavior and feelings are seen as an isolated case, a one-time occurrence, part of a special, never-to-be-repeated relationship: "I never thought of my feelings and our lovemaking as lesbian. The whole experience was too beautiful for it to be something so ugly. I didn't think I could ever have those feelings for another woman" (author's files).

Defining the self as *ambisexual* (bisexual) is another redefinitional strategy: "I guess I'm attracted to both women and men" (author's files). People who adopt *temporary-identity* strategies see their homosexual feelings and behaviors as stages or phases of development that will pass in time: "I'm just passing through a phase, I'm not really homosexual" (author's files). Finally, those who adopt *situational* strategies define the situation, rather than themselves, as responsible for the homosexual activity or feelings: "It only happened because I was drunk"; "It never would have happened if I hadn't been sent to prison."

A fifth overall strategy is *acceptance.* With acceptance, men and women acknowledge that their behavior, feelings, or fantasies may be homosexual, and seek out additional sources of information to determine the nature of their sexual preferences. For adolescent men and women who always felt different because they felt that their thoughts, feelings, and behaviors were at odds with others of their sex, their sense of isolation is diminished by the gradual realization that homosexuals exist as a social category and that they are "probably" homosexual. The homosexual category provides them with a label for their difference. "From the time I was quite young I felt different from other girls and I felt more masculine than feminine. When I learned that lesbians existed I had a word that explained why I was different from other girls" (author's files). "The first name I had for what I was, was 'cocksucker.' 'Cocksucker' was an awful word the way they used it, but it meant that my condition was nameable. I finally had a name for all those feelings. I wasn't nothing" (Reinhart 1982, 26).

Perceptions of self anchored in the strategies of denial, repair, avoidance, or redefinition may be sustained for months or years or permanently. Ambisexual perceptions of self, for example—a redefinitional strategy—may be maintained or undermined by a person's social roles, social structures, and relationships, and by the perceived strength, persistence, and salience of the homosexual feelings. Although individuals may use several different strategies for stigma management, they characteristically use some more than others.

Whether the etiology of homosexuality is anchored in biological predispositions or social learning, "the evidence now available suggests that, at least for some individuals, childhood and adolescent experiences may serve as the basis for adult homosexual identity" (Minton and McDonald 1983/1984, 97).

Stage 3: Identity Assumption

Despite differences in stigma-management strategies, a significant number of men and women progress to *identity assumption,* the third stage of homosexual identity formation, during or after late adolescence. In this stage, the homosexual identity becomes both a self-identity and a presented identity—at least to other homosexuals. Defining the self as homosexual and presenting the self as homosexual to other homosexuals are the first stages in a larger process of identity disclosure called *coming out* (Coleman 1982; Lee 1977). The hallmarks of this stage are self-definition as homosexual; identity tolerance and acceptance, regular association with other homosexuals, sexual experimentation, and exploration of the homosexual subculture.

Homosexual self-definition occurs in contexts that vary between the sexes. Lesbians typically arrive at homosexual self-definitions in contexts of intense affectionate involvements with other women (Cronin 1974; Schäfer 1976). Seventy-six percent of the lesbians interviewed by Cronin, for example, defined themselves in contexts of meaningful emotional involvements with other women. Gay males, in contrast, are more likely to arrive at homosexual self-definitions in social/sexual contexts where men are reputed to gather for sexual purposes—gay bars, parties, parks, YMCAs, and men's rooms (Dank 1971; Troiden 1979; Warren 1974). Only a minority of males appear to define themselves in contexts of same-sex love relationships (Dank 1971; McDonald 1982; Troiden 1979). Today, I suspect that young men are more likely to arrive at homosexual self-definitions in romantic or fantasized contexts than in sexual settings. For many men, the possibility of contracting AIDS has reduced the perceived desirability of sexual experimentation.

Patterns laid down during sex-role socialization explain why lesbians define themselves in emotional contexts, gay males in social/sexual contexts. "Male sexuality is seen as active, initiatory, demanding of immediate gratification, and divorced from emotional attachment; female sexuality emphasizes feelings and minimizes the importance of immediate sexual activity" (de Monteflores and Schultz 1978). For males, admitting a desire for homosexual activity implies the label of homosexual; for females, intense emotional involvement with the same sex has similar implications.

Lesbians and gay males also typically define themselves as homosexual at different ages. Retrospective studies of adult homosexuals suggest that gay males arrive at homosexual self-definitions between the ages of nineteen and twenty-one, on the average (Dank 1971; Harry and Devall 1978; Kooden et al. 1979; McDonald 1982; Troiden 1979). Retrospective studies involving small samples of adolescent gay males indicate a younger age at the time of self-identification as homosexual: age fourteen, on the average (Remafedi 1987). Adult lesbians recall reaching homosexual self-definitions slightly later, between the average ages of twenty-one and twenty-three (Califia 1979; Riddle and Morin 1977; Schäfer 1976; Smith 1980).

Self-definition as homosexual may occur just before, at the same time as, or shortly after first social contact with other homosexuals (Cronin 1974; Dank 1971; Ponse 1978; Troiden 1979). Initial contacts may have been engineered consciously (e.g., by deciding to go to a homosexual bar) or accidentally (e.g., by learning that a friend is homosexual). Only a minority of lesbians and gay males appear to define themselves as homosexual without having direct contact with one or more homosexuals. Self-designation as homosexual in the absence of affiliation with other homosexuals (e.g., as a consequence of reading about homosexuality) has been referred to as *disembodied affiliation* (Ponse 1978).

Although homosexual identities are assumed during this stage, initially they are tolerated rather than accepted. Cass (1984) describes people who tolerate their homosexual identities as follows:

> You feel sure you're a homosexual and you put up with, or tolerate this. You see yourself as a homosexual for now but are not sure about how you will be in the future. You usually take care to put across a heterosexual image. You sometimes mix socially with homosexuals, or would like to do this. You feel a need to meet others like yourself. (p. 156)

Sophie (1985/1986) describes this period as the "testing and exploration" phase of lesbian identity formation.

The quality of a person's initial contacts with homosexuals is extremely important (Cass 1979). If initial contacts are negative, further contact with homosexuals may be avoided and nonhomosexual perceptions of self will persist, maintained through the strategies of denial, repair, self-definition as ambisexual, or temporary identity described earlier. Perceptions of the increased risks of living as a homosexual in a homophobic society, such as blackmail or fear of AIDS, may also encourage individuals to cling to nonhomosexual perceptions of self.

Positive contacts with other homosexuals, on the other hand, facilitate homosexual identity formation. Favorable contacts provide lesbians and gay males with the opportunity to obtain information about homosexuality at first hand. Direct positive exposure provides a basis for re-examining and re-evaluating their own ideas about homosexuality and for seeing similarities between themselves and those labeled "homosexual." The meanings attributed to the homosexual label begin to change in a more favorable direction.

Personally meaningful contacts with experienced homosexuals also enable neophytes to see that homosexuality is socially organized and that a group exists to which they may belong, which diminishes feelings of solitariness and alienation. Other homosexuals provide neophytes with role models from whom they learn strategies for stigma management, rationalizations that legitimize homosexuality and neutralize guilt feelings, the range of identities and roles available to homosexuals, and the norms governing homosexual conduct.

Once they adopt homosexual identities, lesbians and gay males are confronted with the issue of stigma and its management. They may adopt one or several stigma-evasion strategies during identity assumption: capitulation, minstrelization (Levine 1987), passing, or group alignment (Humphreys 1972).

Women and men who *capitulate* avoid homosexual activity because they have internalized a stigmatizing view of homosexuality. The persistence of homosexual feelings in the absence of homosexual activity, however, may lead them to experience self-hatred and despair. In *minstrelization,* individuals express their homosexuality along lines etched out by the popular culture. They behave as the wider culture expects them to behave—in highly stereotyped, gender-inappropriate fashions.

Passing as heterosexual is probably the most common stigma-evasion strategy (Humphreys 1972), especially among recently self-defined homosexuals. Women and men who pass as heterosexual define themselves as homosexual, but conceal their sexual preferences and behavior from heterosexuals—family, friends, and colleagues—"by careful, even torturous, control of information" (Humphreys 1972, 138). Passers lead "double lives"; they segregate their social worlds into heterosexual and homosexual spheres and hope the two never collide.

Group alignment is also adopted commonly by neophyte homosexuals to evade stigma. Men and women who evade stigma through affiliation become actively involved in the homosexual community. The perception of "belonging" to a world of others situated similarly eases the pain of stigma. They look upon other homosexuals as sources of social and emotional support, as well as sexual gratification. Yet an awareness of "belonging" to the homosexual subculture also fosters an awareness of "not belonging," perceptions of being excluded from the worlds of opposite-sex dating, marriage, and parenthood. People may deal with this alienation by *immersing* themselves completely in the homosexual subculture; by *avoiding* heterosexual settings that remind them of their stigma; by *normalizing* their behaviors, that is, minimizing the differences between heterosexuals and homosexuals (Ponse 1978); by *aristocratizing* homosexual behavior, that is, attaching a special significance to homosexual experience (Ponse 1980); or by *nihilizing* heterosexual experience, that is, viewing heterosexual patterns as deviant (Warren 1980).

To recapitulate, positive homosexual experiences facilitate homosexual self-definition, whereas unrewarding experiences reinforce negative attitudes toward homosexuality. Undesirable homosexual experiences may prompt people to reject the identity ("I am really heterosexual"), abandon the behavior ("I want sex with others of the same sex but can get by without it"), or reject both identity and behavior ("I am not homosexual. I can learn to desire the opposite sex").

By the end of the identity assumption stage, people begin to accept themselves as homosexual. Cass (1984) describes *acceptance* of the homosexual identity as follows:

> You are quite sure you are a homosexual and you accept this fairly happily. You are prepared to tell a few people about being a homosexual but you carefully select whom you will tell. You adopt an attitude of fitting in where you live and work. You can't see any point in confronting people with your homosexuality if it's going to embarrass all concerned. (p. 156)

Sophie (1985/1986) also uses the term "identity acceptance" to describe this stage of lesbian identity development.

Stage 4: Commitment

A *commitment* is a feeling of obligation to follow a particular course of action (Theodorson and Theodorson 1969). In the homosexual context, it involves adopting homosexuality as a way of life. For the committed homosexual, "it becomes easier, more attractive, less costly to remain a homosexual" than to try to function as a heterosexual (Plummer 1975, 150). Entering a same-sex love relationship marks the onset of commitment (Coleman 1982; Troiden 1979). The identity assumption and commitment stages described here are incorporated in Minton and McDonald's (1983/1984) "universalistic" stage. Following Cass (1979), Sophie (1985/1986) labels the fourth stage of lesbian identity formation "identity integration."

The hallmarks of the commitment stage are self-acceptance and comfort with the homosexual identity and role. Commitment has both internal and external dimensions. It is indicated *internally* by the fusion of sexuality and emotionality into a significant whole, a shift in the meanings attached to homosexual identities, a perception of the homosexual identity as a valid self-identity, expressed satisfaction with the homosexual identity, and increased happiness following self-definition as homosexual. It is indicated *externally* by same-sex love relationships, disclosure of the homosexual identity to nonhomosexual audiences, and a shift in the kinds of stigma-management strategies.

Internal Indicators. The fusion of same-sex sexuality and emotionality into a meaningful whole is one internal measure of a person's commitment to homosexuality as a way of life (Coleman 1982; Troiden 1979; Warren 1974). The same sex is redefined as a legitimate source of love and romance, as well as sexual gratification. Homosexuals themselves see same-sex romantic preferences as differentiating "true" homosexuals from those who are merely experimenting (Warren 1974).

Another internal measure of commitment to homosexuality as a way of life is reflected by the meanings attached by homosexuals to the homosexual identity. The homosexual subculture encourages both lesbians and gay males (Ponse 1978, 1980; Warren 1974, 1980; Warren and Ponse 1977) to perceive the homosexual identity as an "essential" identity — a state of being and way of life — rather than merely a form of behavior or sexual orientation. Lesbian feminists are especially likely to view lesbianism as all-encompassing: "A lesbian's entire sense of self centers on women. While sexual energies are not discounted, alone they do not create the lesbian feminist" (Faderman 1984/1985, 87).

The perception of the homosexual identity as a valid self-identity is also a sign of internal commitment. Homosexual identities and roles are seen as growing out of genuine, deep-seated needs and desires. Homosexual expression is reconceptualized as "natural" and "normal" for the self. Committed homosexuals find the homosexual identity "a more valid expression of the human condition than that afforded by a heterosexual one" (Humphreys 1979, 242).

The degree of satisfaction that people express about their present identities is another measure of internal commitment (Hammersmith and Weinberg 1973). When Bell and Weinberg (1978) asked their sample of homosexuals whether they would remain homosexual even if a magic pill would enable them to become heterosexual, 95 percent of the lesbians and 86 percent of the gay males claimed they would *not* take the magic pill. In addition, 73 percent of the gay males and 84 percent of the lesbians indicated they had "very little or no" regret about their homosexuality. Only 6 percent of the male and 2 percent of the female homosexuals felt "a great deal" of regret. Societal rejection and punitiveness and the inability to have children were the most frequently mentioned sources of regret.

Increased happiness is another indication of an internal commitment to homosexuality. When asked, "At this time would you say you are more, less, or about as happy as you were prior to arriving at a homosexual self-definition?", 91 percent of the gay males I interviewed indicated they were more happy, 8 percent stated they were about as happy, and only one person said he was less happy (Troiden 1979).

External Indicators. A same-sex love relationship is one external sign of a commitment to homosexuality as a way of life (Coleman 1982; Troiden 1979; Warren 1974), a concrete manifestation of a synthesis of same-sex emotionality and sexuality into a meaningful whole. Lesbians appear to enter their first same-sex love relationships between the ages of twenty-two and twenty-three (Bell and Weinberg 1978; Riddle and Morin 1977), a year or less after they define themselves as lesbians. Gay males typically have their first love affairs between the ages of twenty-one and twenty-four (Bell and Weinberg 1978; McDonald 1982; Troiden 1979), roughly two to five years after they define themselves as homosexual. In keeping with their gender-role training, males are much more likely than lesbians to gain sexual experiences with a variety of partners before focusing their attentions on one special person (Troiden 1979). Lesbians are more likely to explore the homosexual community and gain sexual experiences in the context of an emotional relationship with one other woman, or a series of "special" women (Cronin 1974; Smith 1980).

Disclosure of the homosexual identity to heterosexual audiences is another external measure of commitment to homosexuality as a way of life. As mentioned earlier, coming out involves disclosure of the homosexual identity to some members of an expanding series of audiences ranging from self to other homosexuals, to heterosexual friends and/or family, to co-workers, to employers, and to the general public by self-identification as homosexual through the media (Coleman 1982; Hencken and O'Dowd 1977; Lee 1977).

Homosexual identity formation is characterized over time by an increasing desire to disclose the homosexual identity to nonhomosexual audiences (Cass 1984). Few people, however, disclose their homosexual identities to everybody in their social environments. Instead, they fluctuate "back and forth in degrees of openness, depending on personal, social, and professional factors" (de Monteflores and Schultz 1978). Lesbians and gay males appear more likely to come out to siblings, close heterosexual friends, or parents than to co-workers or employers. Fifty percent of the gay males and 62 percent of the lesbians interviewed by Bell and Weinberg (1978) said they had told "some or all" of their siblings about their homosexuality. Regarding disclosure to heterosexual friends, 54 percent of the lesbians and

53 percent of the gay males claimed that "some or most" of their heterosexual friends knew about their homosexuality. Fewer had told their parents about their homosexuality. Forty-two percent of the gay males and 49 percent of the lesbians said they had come out to their mothers, and 37 percent of the females and 31 percent of the males said they had told their fathers.

Bell and Weinberg's (1978) respondents exercised even greater discretion in disclosing their homosexual identities to co-workers and employers. Sixty-two percent of the gay males and 76 percent of the lesbians stated that "few or none" of their co- workers knew they were homosexual, and 85 percent of the lesbians and 71 percent of the gay males claimed that their employers were unaware of their homosexuality. Lesbians and gay males appear reluctant to come out in the workplace for two reasons: fear of endangering job credibility or effectiveness, and fear of job or income loss (Kooden et al. 1979; Riddle and Morin 1977).

Those lesbians who disclose their homosexual identities to nonhomosexual friends begin to do so at an average age of twenty-eight (Riddle and Morin 1977); gay males begin to disclose their identities between the average ages of twenty-three and twenty- eight (McDonald 1982; Riddle and Morin 1977). Gay males who disclose their homosexual identities to their parents do so at age twenty-eight, on the average; lesbians at an average age of thirty (Riddle and Morin 1977). Those who come out in professional settings do so at even later average ages — thirty-two for lesbians and thirty-one for gay males (Riddle and Morin 1977). The AIDS epidemic has increased the stigma attached to homosexuality. As a result, younger (and older) gay males and lesbians may be less willing today than in the past to disclose their homosexual identities to nonhomosexual audiences.

A third external indicator of commitment is a shift in stigma-management strategies. Covering (Humphreys 1972) and blending appear to replace passing and group alignment as the most common strategies, with a minority opting for conversion (Humphreys 1972).

Women and men who *cover* are ready to admit that they are homosexual (often because it is obvious or known), but nonetheless take great pains to keep their homosexuality from looming large. They manage their homosexuality in ways meant to demonstrate that although they may be homosexual, they are nonetheless respectable. "Imitation of heterosexual marriage, along with other roles and lifestyles designed to elicit praise from the straight segments of society" typifies this form of stigma evasion (Humphreys 1972, 139). Like people who blend, people who cover turn to other homosexuals for social and emotional support as well as sexual gratification, and disclose their homosexual identities selectively to significant heterosexuals.

People who *blend* act in gender-appropriate ways and neither announce nor deny their homosexual identities to nonhomosexual others.

They perceive their sexual preferences as irrelevant to the kinds of activities they undertake with heterosexuals, and cloak their private lives and sexuality in silence. When quizzed or challenged about their sexual preferences or behavior, they are likely to respond: "What's it to you?" or "It's none of your business." Women and men who blend affiliate with the homosexual subculture and present themselves as homosexual to other gay males and lesbians and to carefully selected nonhomosexuals. As used here, blending is similar to Warren's "avoidance without hiding" (1974, 94).

Lesbians and gay males who *convert* acquire an ideology or world view that not only destigmatizes homosexuality but transforms it from a vice to a virtue, from a mark of shame to a mark of pride. People who convert confront rather than evade the homosexual stigma. Formally or informally, they attempt to inform the general public about the realities of homosexuality and the special contributions made to society by homosexuals in hopes of eliminating oppression through education and political change (e.g., equal rights in jobs and housing). A few lesbians and gay males adopt conversionist strategies during the identity assumption stage when they define themselves as homosexual.

Stigma-evasion strategies are situational rather than constant — that is, personal, social, or professional factors may prompt individuals to blend or cover in some situations, disclose their homosexual identity openly in others, and switch to conversionist modes in yet other contexts. Selective and relatively nonselective self-disclosure have important consequences for the self. Identity disclosure enables the homosexual identity to be realized more fully — that is, brought into concrete existence — in a wider range of contexts. A more complete integration between homosexuals' identities and their social worlds is made possible when they can see and present themselves as homosexual and can be viewed as such by others. *Identity synthesis,* associated with identity disclosure, is described by Cass (1984) in the following way:

> You are prepared to tell [almost] *anyone* that you are a homosexual. You are happy about the way you are but feel that being a homosexual is not the most important part of you. You mix socially with homosexuals and heterosexuals [with whom] you are open about your homosexuality. (p. 156)

The passage of time also forges links between many social situations and identities, which accounts partly for the stability of adult identities. By the time individuals reach middle age, the people with whom they routinely interact have a huge backlog of evidence about what they are like, and should be like, in a variety of roles and situations (Atchley 1982). It becomes increasingly difficult to misrepresent oneself to intimates and co-workers. Moreover, as time passes,

> people tend to conclude that they know themselves as well and probably better than anyone else does or could. This can lead us to assign more weight to what we think about ourselves than to what others say about us. We may also feel that stereotypes about some category we might be assigned to are irrelevant to our own self images. (Atchley 1982, 383)

Commitment to the homosexual identity and role is a matter of degree. Homosexuals span a continuum from low to high levels of commitment on both internal and external dimensions, which may vary across time and place. For this reason, commitment is always somewhat inconsistent, strengthened or weakened at various points and contexts by personal, social, or professional factors.

Conclusions

In the final analysis, homosexual identity is emergent — never fully determined in a fixed or absolute sense, but always subject to modification and further change. Homosexual identity formation is continuous, a process of "becoming" that spans a lifetime, a process of "striving but never arriving" (Plummer 1975). The rates of homosexual identity formation, however, may be influenced by a number of factors, which serve as qualifications to the model.

Homosexual events are well defined, clearly recognizable occurrences in the lives of women and men who define themselves as homosexual and adopt homosexuality as a way of life. As indicated earlier, these events (or components of homosexual experience) are often clustered with the various stages. Examples of homosexual events include first awareness of same-sex attraction, first homosexual activity, self-definition as homosexual, first association with other homosexuals, and first same-sex love relationship.

The average ages for the homosexual events reported here were obtained from only a few studies; further replications are necessary. Until more investigations have been conducted, these average ages should be viewed as educated guesses.

Sample characteristics have been shown to influence rates of homosexual identity formation and the reported ages for the homosexual events; the mean ages of respondents in the studies cited here vary, for example. In samples consisting of relatively older lesbians and gay males, the respondents recall that they encountered the various events at relatively higher average ages than younger informants, thus raising the average ages at which the events seem to occur. Older informants grew up during a time when homosexuality was rarely discussed, and then only in highly stereotypical terms.

Research conducted in the 1970s and 1980s indicates that adolescent lesbians and gay males in the United States may encounter the events and acquire their homosexual identities at earlier ages than did their older counterparts. More specifically, homosexuals under twenty-five may encounter the various components of homosexual identity at significantly lower average ages than those reported here. Increased openness, tolerance, and accurate information about homosexuality in the United States may have made it easier to perceive similarities between self and "homosexuals" (Dank 1971; Remafedi 1987; Troiden 1977, 1979; Troiden and Goode 1980).

On the other hand, the onset of the AIDS epidemic may have the opposite effect on homosexual identity formation; it may delay the process (at least among males) because AIDS has increased the stigma attached to homosexuality. The possibility of contracting AIDS may motivate people defensively to deny their erotic feelings, to delay acting on them, or to express them only in the context of a committed love relationship. In addition, the AIDS crisis may undermine identity integration and a positive sense of homosexual identity. To avoid being seen as potential disease carriers, lesbians and gay males may choose not to disclose their homosexual identities to nonhomosexual audiences. Identity fear may replace identity pride; fears of infection may promote erotophobia — the fear of sexual relations — and cause people to avoid homosexual behavior completely or reduce their sexual experimentation.

Gender-inappropriate behavior (Harry 1982), adolescent homosexual arousal and activity, and an absence of heterosexual experiences (Troiden and Goode 1980) may also facilitate progress through the events and stages. Gender-atypical, homosexually active, heterosexually inexperienced lesbians and gay males may experience less identity confusion than other homosexuals to the extent that gender conventions in American society articulate linkages between adult homosexuality and all three of these characteristics. Conversely, gay males and lesbians who are gender-typical, heterosexually active, and homosexually inexperienced may experience more confusion regarding their sexual identities because their characteristics are at variance with prevailing homosexual stereotypes.

Supportive family and friends may also facilitate homosexual identity formation. Individuals may feel more comfortable in acting upon their sexual feelings when they believe that those close to them will accept them as they are. Conversely, lesbians and gay males with nonsupportive families and friends may find it much more difficult to acknowledge and act upon their sexual feelings. Fears of rejection appear to inhibit homosexual identity formation to various degrees.

Educational level and the prevailing atmosphere of the workplace may also facilitate or hinder homosexual identity formation. Highly educated lesbians and gay males in homophobic professions may fear that they have more to lose by acknowledging and acting upon their sexual feelings than their less highly educated counterparts. Fears of job or income loss, or concerns about endangering professional credibility, appear to inhibit homosexual identity formation (Kooden et al. 1979; Riddle and Morin 1977; Troiden 1977). Less educationally specialized lesbians and gay males and those who work in more supportive occupations may not perceive themselves as occupationally at risk by acting upon and integrating their sexual feelings into their overall lives.

In Chapters 5, 6, and 7, I familiarize the reader with competing sociological perspectives on the nature of homosexuality and homosexual identity. The social-role, social-construction, and sex-orientation perspectives have emerged during the past decade; they differ in focus, conceptualization of homosexual identity, and key explanatory concepts.

5 THE SOCIAL-ROLE
PERSPECTIVE

During the past decade, sociological discourse on homosexual identity
has evolved from three general orientations toward homosexuality: the
social-role and social-construction positions, which overlap considerably,
and the essentialist approach, which is more clinical than the other two
(Plummer 1981a, 94). Sociologists who study homosexuality commonly
alternate between the social-role and social-construction positions, depending on the topics investigated. From time to time, scholars also adopt an
essentialist stance.

This chapter discusses the social-role perspective and highlights its
distinguishing features. The earmarks of the social-role approach to
homosexuality include the use of the term homosexual; the view of "the
homosexual" as a social type; the description of how homosexual roles are
learned; the focus on the presented dimension of homosexual identity; and
the explanation of the stability of homosexual identities and roles over
time.

Use of the Term Homosexual

The related concepts of status and role dominate social-role discussions
of homosexuality and the meanings attributed to the term *homosexual.*
Homosexual self-typing involves more than adopting a new (and stigmatized)
self-identity; it also involves a shift in social location, or *status.* In the after-
math of self-labeling, the self occupies a different social structural position – the "homosexual" position.

Role is the dynamic aspect of status, and the expected pattern of
behavior associated with the homosexual status is the *homosexual role.*
Homosexual status is expressed when individuals play out the homosexual
role, as defined by the wider culture. Historically, both the homosexual
status and the homosexual role have been held in disregard in the United
States and Great Britain.

From a social-role perspective, the word *homosexual* is used as an adjective to describe sexual experiences involving the same sex. These same-
sex experiences may involve sexual behaviors, fantasies, or feelings. As an

adjective, homosexual suggests what people do, think, or feel, not what they are. It describes activity — a role — rather than a specific quality or state of being (Gagnon and Simon 1973; Omark 1979, 1981a, 1981b; Plummer 1981a, 1981b; Richardson 1983/1984; Sagarin 1973, 1975, 1976, 1979).

From this perspective, becoming homosexual is no different from becoming a doctor, a secretary, a chef, or a tennis player. People learn to be homosexual just as they learn anything else; they may or may not carry this preference into the future, or have had it in the past. Homosexuality is what someone *does* — a behavior — not something that one *is* in a fixed, essential sense (Omark 1979, 1981b; Plummer 1981a, 1981b; Sagarin 1973, 1975, 1976, 1979).

Homosexual as Social Type

According to supporters of the social-role perspective, the view that people are sexually of one nature or the other (heterosexual or homosexual) is specific to history and culture. Social-role adherents marshal the results of historical and anthropological research, including the concepts of polymorphous perversity, homosexualities, and the heterosexual/homosexual continuum, to support the position that homosexuality is a behavior rather than an essence.

Historical Evidence

A major flaw in the "homosexuality as condition" argument is apparent in historical investigations of homosexuality. The idea that there are two kinds of people — heterosexual and homosexual — and that homosexuality is a condition that individuals have or lack has been traced to intellectual traditions that emerged in the West during the past 200 years (Richardson 1983/1984). Before the nineteenth century, homosexuality was treated as sinful or degenerate behavior. Nevertheless, its practitioners were not thought to differ internally from nonpractitioners.

From the social-role perspective, what it means to be homosexual and what a homosexual "is" are specific to culture and history:

In different cultures (and at different historical moments or conjunctures within the same culture) very different meanings are given to same-sex activity both by society at large and by the individual participants. The physical acts might be similar, but the social construction of meanings around them are profoundly different. The social integration of forms of pedagogic homosexual relations in ancient Greece have no continuity with contemporary notions of homosexual identity. (Weeks 1981, 81)

The homosexual role is more than a pattern of sexual behavior; it does not merely outline how people interact sexually with others of the same sex. Roles are stereotypical. They represent summarized sets of expectations about the characteristics of those who occupy certain social positions. Preconceived notions about how homosexuals act and what they are like as people vary across history and cultures, as well as within a given culture (Davies 1984).

Americans assume that homosexuals have always exhibited exclusively homosexual desires and behaviors. In addition, according to sociologist Mary McIntosh (1968), they expect that homosexual men will be

effeminate in manner, personality, or preferred sexual activity: the expectation that sexuality will play a part of some kind in all of his relations with other men; and the expectation that he will be attracted to boys and very young men and probably willing to seduce them. (p. 185)

The idea that male homosexuals possess behavioral characteristics that distinguish them from heterosexuals emerged in England during the late seventeenth century. During this period, descriptions of men who engaged in homosexual behavior mentioned more frequently than today the characteristics of transvestism and effeminacy. By the late nineteenth century, sexual promiscuity was added to the list of expected behaviors. At that time, the idea that homosexuals differ from heterosexuals internally as well as behaviorally began to emerge. "Homosexual" states of mind, as well as activities, began to be stigmatized.

Until recently, adequate data on lesbianism were hard to find in the historical record. Lillian Faderman (1981), however, has documented the existence and widespread practice of "romantic friendships" between women in the eighteenth century that sometimes included same-sex experiences. "Only if the women started to cross-dress and 'act like men' was it taken as a threat to the male world and hence reacted to with vengeance" (Plummer 1984, 225).

Jeffrey Weeks (1981) states that homosexuality came to be seen as a distinct condition or quality of being during the latter part of the nineteenth century. He points out that the term *homosexuality* was not invented until 1869 when Karoly Benkert, a Hungarian, coined the word. It did not enter into English usage until the 1880s and 1890s when it was introduced by Havelock Ellis, a British sexologist.

Moral and legal reforms in the late nineteenth century had sparked a "scientific" interest in understanding sexuality in hopes of eliminating sexual variations, especially prostitution and homosexual behavior. In attempting to explain homosexual behavior, these early medical and psychiatric writings created a new social category, "homosexual," and elaborated specific criteria for determining the presence of the "condition." Criteria included the already-mentioned traits of effeminacy, promiscuity, and cross-sex dressing (McIntosh 1968), along with an "inability to whistle, penchant for the color green, adoration of mother or father, and [early] age of sexual maturation" (Weeks 1981, 83).

At the beginning of the twentieth century, the notion that homosexuality represented a state of being gave way to the narrower view that homosexuality indicated a specific state of sexual desire (Richardson 1983/1984). The aim and direction of sexual desire came to be used increasingly as a means of differentiating homosexuals from heterosexuals. Revisionist psychoanalytical thought ushered in a further shift in emphasis: Sexual desire was recast as a lifelong orientation, a preference organized in a relatively fixed and unchanging fashion, rather than the outcome of undifferentiated instinctual forces (Richardson 1983/1984).

From a twentieth-century medical/analytic perspective, homosexual desire became the criterion used to indicate the "homosexual" condition or orientation. Homosexual behavior was viewed as an unambiguous indicator of an erotic preference for the same sex, and it became medicalized—that is, likened to a disease—and interpreted as a symptom of "mental illness."

Behaviorism, which emphasizes observable behaviors and avoids the psychoanalytic preoccupation with "states of mind," assumed that homosexual behavior and desire go hand in hand; that homosexual behavior is a reliable indicator of the homosexual condition; and that the condition can be treated with behavior modification (operant conditioning) techniques (Richardson 1983/1984).

The medical model of homosexuality as a form of mental disease went unchallenged until the mid-1950s, when Evelyn Hooker's (1957, 1958) pioneering study of matched samples of heterosexuals and homosexuals failed to reveal significant differences between the two groups in level of psychological functioning. The American Psychiatric Association removed ego-syntonic (self-accepting) homosexuality from its list of mental disorders in 1974, after other investigations yielded similar results (Evans 1970; Freedman 1971; Green 1972; Hopkins 1969; Saghir and Robins 1973; Siegelman 1972; Thompson et al. 1971). Thus "the homosexual" has been reconstituted so that he or she now falls within the normal range of psychological functioning.

In summary, from a social-role perspective, homosexuality is viewed as an essence because it has been defined as such, not because homosexuals differ from nonhomosexuals in essential ways. The homosexual "condition" is a social type or social construction used to differentiate people on the basis of sexual behavior, which is organized and expressed through sexual scripts (roles).

Anthropological Evidence

Anthropological evidence gives further support to the argument that homosexuality represents a social construction rather than an essential condition. The ideas of what a homosexual "is," and what it "means" to be homosexual, vary between cultures and across time.

Systems of kinship and economy, age, and gender influence the way cultures construct lesbianism and male homosexuality. Kinship systems exert an especially potent influence on the routinization of lesbianism and male homosexuality:

> The ethnographic literature reveals that same-sex bonds typically conform to the same kinship codes that arrange other aspects of life. When homosexual desire is routinized, it attains a place and meaning consistent with overall kinship logic. Similarly, different kinship structures create their own fields of eroticism and thus particular sets of occasions for sexualized relations between people, whether of different or the same sexes. (Adam 1985, 20)

Images of lesbians and expectations surrounding lesbian roles are embedded in notions of kinship, which is generally linked in some fashion to the structure of female activities and associations:

> Women in all cultures are expected to marry and bear children; in many they are betrothed and wed before or soon after puberty. Consequently, for the most part lesbian behavior locates within the structure of marriage relations, but within that system a variety of sexual relations are possible. (Blackwood 1985, 11)

Among the socially egalitarian Australian aborigines, for example, adolescent lesbian relations played an integral role in the kinship system. A girl entered into a lesbian relationship with her female cross-cousin, "whose family would later give her their son to marry, the girl-friends thereby becoming sisters-in-law" (Blackwood 1985, 11). (Cross-cousins are children of opposite-sex siblings.)

Social stratification (which encompasses the economic dimension) also shapes the social construction of lesbianism:

> In societies where women have control over their productive activities and status, both formal and informal relations may occur. Where women lack power, particularly in class societies, they maintain only informal lesbian ties or build institutions outside the dominant culture. (Blackwood 1985, 10)

Evelyn Blackwood finds it useful to typologize the social contexts in which cross-cultural lesbian behavior occurs as ranging from the informal to the formal. Informal relations between women do not extend beyond the current situation (e.g., the adolescent sex play among women in harems). Formal relations, in contrast, involve same-sex activity that extends beyond the pair and is part of a larger social structure or network (e.g., initiation schools, bond friendship, sisterhoods).

Several patterns of formal and informal lesbian relations emerge in nonclass societies where women have greater autonomy. Among the polygynous Azande of Africa, for example, where each wife had her own dwelling and her own plot of land, and controlled whatever profits from her work she made through trade, some women established lesbian relationships with their co-wives within the formal structure of polygynous marriage. Husbands could not forbid these arrangements, but the wives kept them secret to avoid threatening their husbands (Blackwood 1985). Lesbian relationships are also reported to exist between co-wives of the Nyakyusa, another polygynous African group (Adam 1985).

In class societies, where women lack autonomy and power, formal lesbian relationships, if they exist at all, occupy a marginal status in relation to the dominant culture. In the Near East, for example, lesbian behavior among women in harems and within the Muslim institution of purdah was clandestine and informal. Homosexual behavior is outlawed under Islamic law, and adultery is punishable by divorce or death (Blackwood 1985).

The ethnographic evidence suggests that age-structured homosexuality among unmarried male youths is extremely common in societies where "bachelorhood" is a transitional status between childhood and adulthood. Among the Nyakyusa, for example, young males between the ages of ten or eleven and twenty-five separate from their families to form peer groups that set up entirely new villages for themselves. "It is generally accepted that these youths engage in reciprocal homosexual relations, including sleeping and dancing together erotically" (Adam 1985, 21). Homosexual relations are expected to cease once they marry. Lesbian relations among the Australian aborigines also illustrate the peer-oriented model. In these cases, exclusively homosexual youth become exclusively heterosexual adults.

Ritualized homosexual relations between older males and younger males are even more common and provide a contrast to the peer-oriented models described above. These relationships fall into two major categories: the *ancient model* and the *Melanesian model* (Adam 1985).

In the ancient model, an older married male enters into a role-structured pedagogic/sexual relationship with a young man. The older man socializes the youth to male culture and gender functions. A role differentiation consistent with this "one-way" socialization emerges: The older man is the provider and the younger man is the recipient, and this differentiation "structures anal and oral intercourse" (Adam 1985, 22). The ancient Greeks and the Etoro of New Guinea exhibit this pattern (Dover 1978; Kelly 1976). In the ancient model, an exclusively homosexual youth becomes a bisexual adult by acquiring wives and youthful lovers.

In cultures that adopt the ancient model, the social categories of heterosexual, homosexual, and bisexual are basically meaningless and irrelevant. The fundamental social division in these societies is between "the free, adult male citizen, and all others. Sexuality is merely one of many rights exercised by the free male over women, youths, and slaves" (Adam 1985, 22).

In the Melanesian model, older bachelors enter into role-structured sexual relationships with younger boys. "Gender ideology plays the preeminent role in determining sexuality among males" (Adam 1985, 22). Homosexuality is associated with gender differentiation (masculinization of the male) rather than gender mixing (effeminization of the male), a view that prevails in the contemporary United States. Sexuality is only one of many ways in which males set themselves apart from women and perpetuate the male group. Ritualized homosexuality among the Sambia illustrates the Melanesian model.

"Sambia" is a pseudonym used to protect the identity of a tribe located in Papua, New Guinea (Herdt 1981). Among the Sambia, relations between the sexes are infused with ambivalence. Men see women both as necessary and valuable, and as defiling and threatening. "Most of the personal world is gender-charged; men and women have separate residences, pathways, crops, foods, and rites" (Adam 1985, 25). This uneasiness extends to heterosexuality itself, which is viewed as necessary, even pleasurable, but extremely dangerous. Vaginal secretions and menstrual blood are believed to be polluting, perhaps lethal. Males undergo purgative rites to rid themselves of female contamination after heterosexual contacts. Ritualized male homosexuality, as well as the consumption of male-identified foods and herbs, are constructed culturally as vital to the creation of strength, biological maleness, and masculinity (Herdt 1981).

At approximately age seven, boys are separated from the "polluting" influence of their mothers. For the next ten to fifteen years, they engage daily in ritualized homosexual fellatio, first as the fellators, later as the fellated. The daily ingestion of semen is believed to be absolutely vital to the creation of biological maleness and masculinity. All men take part in this routinized homosexuality, which is hidden from women and lasts into marriage, ending with the onset of biological fatherhood. Among the Sambia, "masculinity is thus a product of a regimen of ritualized homosexuality leading into manhood" (Herdt 1981, 3). Sambian females need not undergo an analogous ritual because they are believed to be essentially female, inherently feminine, and reproductively competent at birth. In the Melanesian model, exclusively homosexual youths become bisexual for a short time during young adulthood (after marriage but before fatherhood), and exclusively heterosexual as adults.

In summary, the social-role approach views "the homosexual" as a social type or construct rather than a distinct species of being. Social, cultural, and historical forces, rather than inherent traits or essences, shape or construct the characteristics thought to correspond to homosexuality and its manner of expression. The term *homosexual* describes a role, an expected pattern of behavior that flows along lines shaped by age, gender conceptions, economic arrangements, and especially kinship. It is a shorthand summary of how a given culture at a given historical point expects homosexually experienced people to be cognitively, emotionally, and behaviorally.

Polymorphous Perversity

The notion of polymorphous perversity (introduced in Chapter 2) is also used to support the claim that homosexuality is a behavior and a role, and thus is learned like anything else. According to this view, homosexuality and heterosexuality have essentially the same, rather than different, roots. Both preferences are learned socially and originate in a generalized sexual pleasure-seeking potential that is present at birth. The foundations for homosexual or heterosexual preferences are laid down during gender-role socialization and are further shaped, channeled, and organized during the process of learning sexual scripts.

Gay males, in keeping with their gender-role socialization, express their sexualities in active, initiatory, genitally focused, goal-oriented ways. By contrast, lesbians frame their sexualities in reactive, emotionally focused, process-oriented ways. Gay males, for example, have homosexual relations with a larger number of partners, more frequently, and at younger ages than lesbians (Bell and Weinberg 1978; Blumstein and Schwartz 1983). They are also less likely than lesbians to remain monogamous in their love-based unions (Blumstein and Schwartz 1983). Similar differences between the sexes are mirrored among heterosexuals (Tavris and Wade 1984).

In keeping with the idea of polymorphous perversity, research suggests that homosexuality is a multidimensional phenomenon and a matter of degree on any given dimension. Depending on the criteria used, an individual may be classified as homosexual along some dimensions but not along others. From a role perspective, who and what a homosexual "is" depends on how, why, when, and where people are classified.

Alfred Kinsey and his associates were the first to demonstrate that human sexual responsiveness and behaviors span a continuum from complete heterosexuality through complete homosexuality. According to the Kinsey team (1948), homosexual/heterosexual distinctions are an arbitrary means of categorizing people:

> The living world is a continuum in each and every one of its aspects. The sooner we learn this concerning human sexual behavior the sooner we shall reach a sound understanding of the realities of sex. (p. 639)

According to the Kinsey et al. (1948) study of sexuality in the human male, over one-third (37%) of all American males have at least one homosexual experience to orgasm between the onset of adolescence (age sixteen) and the onset of old age (age fifty-five). An additional 13 percent of the Kinsey sample said they had been aroused physically by another man without actually engaging in homosexual behavior. Nearly 60 percent of the sample said they had engaged in preadolescent sex play with another boy. Only about 3 or 4 boys in 100 were exclusively homosexual, that is, had never experienced opposite-sex contacts.

Thirty percent of the male sample reported at least incidental homosexual contact or desires during a period of at least three years after the beginning of adolescence; 18 percent had at least as much homosexual as heterosexual activity and/or desire over a period of at least three years; 13 percent had more homosexual than heterosexual experience for a period of at least three years during their lives; and 8 percent were exclusively homosexual for three or more years.

An analogous study of sexuality in the human female reveals a parallel picture for lesbians, although the numbers are considerably smaller. Kinsey et al. (1953) found, for example, that 13 percent of all American women had at least one homosexual experience to orgasm after the onset of adolescence. An additional 7 percent had engaged in at least one homosexual episode after the onset of adolescence, but without orgasm. Only about 1 or 2 females in 100 could be regarded as exclusively homosexual.

Current research continues to support the contention that homosexual/ heterosexual distinctions are an arbitrary means of categorizing people. Evidence still indicates that people tagged as homosexual at any given point in their lives constitute a diverse group whose sexual behavior and feelings are as flexible as they are static.

Bell and Weinberg (1978, 54-58) found considerable variation among homosexuals when they asked their sample of lesbians and gay males to rate their sexual feelings. Forty-two percent of the white homosexual males, 55 percent of the black homosexual males, 38 percent of the black homosexual females, and 50 percent of the white homosexual females in their sample did not rate their sexual feelings as exclusively homosexual.

Similar variability was found when respondents were asked to indicate whether they had ever experienced heterosexual arousal. Seventy-nine percent of the white and 80 percent of the black homosexual females reported heterosexual arousal, and 84 percent of the black and 72 percent of the white homosexual males reported at least one instance of heterosexual arousal.

Although a majority of both sexes viewed themselves as exclusively homosexual in their adult sexual behavior (as indicated in Chapter 4), substantial majorities of both sexes had experienced heterosexual arousal and behavior during adolescence. Similar variations were found by Harry and DeVall (1978, 54); slightly less than half (49%) of the gay males they questioned thought of themselves as exclusively homosexual. An additional 10 percent saw themselves as equally or more heterosexual than homosexual, and 41 percent thought of themselves as predominately homosexual, incidentally heterosexual.

From a social-role perspective, in summary, the term *homosexual* describes a social role and a pattern of activity, not an inherent trait, quality, or essence. The term represents instead a rough scheme for describing the sexual behavior and feelings of a diverse group of individuals. People who have had homosexual experiences differ in the strength of their sexual responsiveness to the same sex, the frequency with which they express it, their willingness to define themselves as homosexual, and their commitment to homosexuality as a way of life. Homosexuals differ from heterosexuals in degree — position on the Kinsey continuum — rather than in kind, namely, in their prevalent choice of sexual partner (Gagnon and Simon 1973).

Learning the Homosexual Role

The social-role position acknowledges that the inclination to engage in homosexual behavior is probably acquired before or during the time when an individual understands what homosexuality is and what it means to be homosexual (Goode 1981a, 1981b). Homosexual roles do not cause homosexual behavior in the first place (Omark 1978a, 1981a); people learn first what it means to be homosexual from the viewpoint of the stigmatizing society, whether or not they eventually adopt homosexual roles.

> Prior to actually engaging in homosexual behavior, one learns what the homosexual role entails — however warped or inaccurate the perception may be. Homosexuality is not a role one *learns* from conventionals; it is a role that one *learns about.* (Goode 1981a, 56)

The Role as Defined Subculturally

From an interactionist perspective, the term *deviance* refers to behavior that stands a high probability of being condemned if witnessed or known about (Goode 1984). Deviance resides in audience judgments or reactions, not in the act itself or inside the actor.

People who are inclined to deviate, that is, engage in behavior that is likely to be condemned, engage in a process of *deviance disavowal* before (or while) they learn the deviant role and acquire corresponding identities. Deviance disavowal involves redefining a socially condemned behavior or condition as normal, and mainstream society's disapproval of it as invalid (Goode 1984). Deviant subcultures assist people in their efforts at deviance disavowal.

A *subculture* is a "normative system of some group or groups smaller than the whole society" (Wolfgang and Ferracuti 1967, 139). Subcultures provide their members with a *vocabulary of motives,* verbal justifications, which allow them to rationalize, redefine as normal, and defend behaviors and identities that are saturated with public scorn (Cressey 1953; Mills 1940). Subcultural support also enables individuals to maintain their self-esteem in the face of public opprobrium.

Subcultures meet the needs of their members in other ways as well. Members of a subculture interact face to face and spend a large part of their time socializing together. In addition to meeting social needs, such interactions facilitate deviance disavowal by providing members with a world view and a group identity that support their unconventional behavior.

Subcultures also exhibit relatively distinctive sets of values; some of the larger culture's values are magnified, and others are de-emphasized. In addition, they generate specialized vocabularies and means of self-expression. Perhaps most important, they provide people with the knowledge and skills they will need to function effectively as members of the group (Humphreys and

Miller 1980). In short, the subculture provides the neophyte with a culture, a world view (ideology), a group identity, and specialized knowledge and skills.

Generally speaking, at least two homosexual roles are learned: the role as perceived by the conventional society, and the role as conceived by members of the homosexual community. The role that mainstream society assigns to homosexuals is learned about during childhood. By contrast, knowledge of the homosexual role, as defined subculturally and enacted by members of the homosexual community, is usually acquired during adolescence or at some point thereafter, when more experienced homosexuals are encountered. Each version of the homosexual role influences the expectations and behavior of homosexuals (and heterosexuals), although the contents of the two roles differ.

The homosexual role as perceived by the wider culture probably exerts a strong influence on an individual's behavior at first contact with the homosexual subculture. The conventional view is more familiar than the subcultural, and has yet to be challenged by direct experience with seasoned members of the homosexual community. Gagnon and Simon (1973) note, for example, that a large proportion of young men adopt highly effeminate mannerisms and act in a stereotypically effeminate fashion during their initial excursions into the homosexual community. In a similar vein, research on lesbianism (Ponse 1980; Smith 1980; Stanley and Wolfe 1980) reveals that some lesbians recall perceiving the need to adopt "butch" or "femme" self-presentational styles when they first came out. For both gay males and lesbians, exposure to insiders' conceptions of the homosexual role usually leads them to modify or abandon their stereotypic styles. Although a uniform perception of the homosexual role does not exist among homosexuals as a group, many homosexual women and men learn through experience that heterosexual society's portrait of homosexual roles is largely inaccurate.

The Diversity of Homosexual Roles

Denyse Lockard (1985) argues that the advent of women's and gay liberation in the 1960s fostered the growth of numerous institutions within the lesbian community and a corresponding diversity among its members. She identifies several features of the lesbian community that facilitate the development and expression of lesbian roles and identities. This community, which consists of diverse "social networks of lesbians" (1985, 84), functions to provide settings in which "women learn and share the feminist-based values of the lesbian subculture," and it develops and maintains institutions that provide "places and structures for lesbian interaction" (1985,

84, 94). Through participation in these social networks and institutions, women develop personal and group identities based on, but not limited to, their sexual preferences.

Humphreys and Miller (1980) also comment at length on the diversity of lifestyles and roles currently available to homosexuals. They believe it is most accurate to describe the homosexual subculture as a *satellite culture* consisting of varied occupational subcultures and "scenes." They define satellite culture as a "cultural entity that has become so extensive and diverse that it spawns subcultures of its own" (Humphreys and Miller 1980, 148). Although most subcultures form around occupations, especially those that demand communication of job-related skills and high levels of interaction among colleagues, some subcultures develop around stigmatized behavior that is group-based, such as juvenile delinquency, prostitution, homosexuality, and illegal drug use.

Gay and lesbian teachers' groups, lesbian and gay merchant associations, homosexual prostitutes, lesbian and gay caucuses within professional associations, and lesbian and gay people in the "business of style" — designers, beauticians, dog groomers, home restorers, and antique dealers — are examples of occupational subcultures that have emerged in the homosexual satellite culture (Humphreys and Miller 1980).

Scenes are cultural units that spring up around recreational activities and have clearly delineated territories. They have

> distinctive, if partial, sets of values, a high degree of differential association, and an argot that helps members identify each other. Members support and train novices in special skills that are somewhat avocational in nature. (Humphreys and Miller 1980, 144)

Examples of scenes within the homosexual community include *cruising scenes* — bars, baths, public toilets, parks, and rest stops, where interaction is erotic and organized around personal or impersonal sex; *social scenes,* which may be elegant (e.g., formal dining and entertainment), down-to-earth (e.g., informal dining and entertainment), or staged to attract a specific crowd (e.g., "leather" or "disco"); *sport scenes,* such as lesbian or gay baseball, football, bowling, or "Olympic" teams; and *community scenes,* made up of political, religious, or self-help organizations.

To recapitulate, competing definitions of the homosexual role inside the gay satellite culture provide individuals with alternative conceptions of the homosexual role. Each occupational subculture and scene within the gay community generates its own vision of what it means to be homosexual. Exposure to the lesbian and gay communities gives individuals a chance to see how the homosexual role is defined by the occupational subcultures and scenes with which they identify. Similarly, the occupational structures and scenes that command their loyalty and interest also color their views of what is involved in sexual expression with others of the same sex.

Homosexual Scripts

Homosexual behavior is a core dimension of the homosexual role. Individuals learn how to interact sexually as well as socially with others of the same sex while they acquire their homosexual roles. As with the social aspects of homosexual roles, each occupational subculture and scene also articulates its own version of what occurs during erotic interactions with the same sex. Norms governing sexual interactions between males immersed in the "leather" scene, for example, differ from those guiding the erotic behaviors of men in the "couples" scene (Lee 1978).

Homosexual erotic conduct is organized and channeled through *homosexual scripts* (Omark 1978b), which guide sexual (rather than social) interaction between persons of the same sex. More specifically, they dictate appropriate and inappropriate sex partners, proper and improper behavior, acceptable and unacceptable timing, permissible and nonpermissible settings, positively and negatively sanctioned motives, and appropriate and inappropriate sexual technique.

Thus, from the social-role perspective, an individual forms his or her conception of the homosexual role from three sources: (1) information or misinformation articulated by the wider society; (2) affiliation with various occupational subcultures and scenes within the homosexual satellite culture; and (3) individual differences — an individual's own perception of the homosexual role as influenced by his or her social-psychological needs and resources. Once people develop a conception of the homosexual role that is consistent with their life situations, their conception of the role is modified further by actual practice. Some ideas and behavior work, others do not. What works at one time, may or may not be useful in another situation or point in time.

The relation between roles and identities is interactive. From the social-role perspective, identity and role learning go hand in hand (Brim 1960; Goode 1984). Involvement with an activity increases the odds (but does not determine) that a person will self-define in terms of the activity. Viewing the self as "being" an outgrowth of an activity will, in turn, foster deeper commitment to the behavior. Thus social and sexual interactions (role behavior) with other homosexuals encourage, but do not mandate, homosexual self-typing in individuals with homosexual inclinations. Homosexual self-definition (identity), in turn, fosters further involvement with homosexual behavior.

Homosexual Identity as Presented Identity

In Chapter 2 I noted that the homosexual identity exists at three levels: as a self-identity, as a presented identity, and as a perceived identity. The homosexual identity is a self-identity when people see themselves as homosexual in relation to sexual or romantic situations. It is a presented identity when people present themselves openly as homosexual in specific social settings. It is a perceived identity when other people look upon individuals as homosexual.

The social-role perspective views identity as grounded in specific social contexts. Normative structures governing activity in specific contexts determine which roles and identities may be expressed legitimately. Situations place limits on the identities and roles that may be enacted appropriately. People usually do not present an "angry spouse" identity and role in church or synagogue, for example; the norms governing conduct in "worship" situations discourage this behavior.

The social-role perspective focuses primarily on the social or presented dimension of identity: how a person presents himself or herself in a given situation, and how situations limit the array of available identities and roles (Burke 1945; Goffman 1959, 1963; Omark 1979, 1981b; Rainwater 1970; Sagarin 1973, 1975, 1976, 1979; Stone 1962). In this context, homosexual identities are not perceived as entering most (or even all) interactions (Omark 1979, 1981b; Sagarin 1973, 1975, 1976, 1979). The social-role viewpoint insists that an image of oneself as "being" homosexual (or heterosexual) in the sense of an identity varies among individuals, across situations, and over time.

According to the social-role perspective, an identity is described as *manifest* when the immediate context permits its corresponding role to be performed; it is *latent* when the situation forbids it to be presented and expressed. Analytically speaking, self-concept consists of a bundle of identities (Omark 1981b; Troiden 1984/1985). Most of these identities are latent most of the time; only a few are offered as currency during any specific interaction (Omark 1981b; Troiden 1984/1985).

The social-role perspective treats the homosexual identity as an identity to be mobilized or set forth only in situations whose norms permit it to be presented — an important function provided by the various subcultures and scenes that make up the homosexual satellite culture. Homosexual identity may also be experienced (but not presented) when sexual or romantic elements are introduced into otherwise ordinary and conventional settings. The experience of homosexual identity may be triggered, for example, when an individual hears co-workers discussing their love affairs openly or making jokes about homosexuals during coffee breaks.

From a social-role perspective, a person "is" homosexual only in situations that honor homosexual conduct and allow him or her to claim the identity and express the corresponding role, although the experience of homosexual identity may be triggered when homosexual elements are introduced into conventional settings (Troiden 1984/1985). The homosexual identity ceases to be relevant, and becomes latent, when an individual leaves homosexual settings for more conventional surroundings.

The most extreme statement of the social-role position is expressed by sociologist Edward Sagarin (1973, 1975, 1976, 1979). He points out that many people have homosexual desires but that relatively few individuals translate these desires into behavior; fewer yet define themselves as homosexual in the sense of a self-identity. He argues that people commit the fallacy of *reification* when they define themselves as "being" what they "do."

Reification is a logical error that involves treating an idea or concept as if it were a definite, concrete object (Goode 1973). People do many different things and possess myriad talents; to single out one or two attributes or behaviors from this vast array and say "I am this or that" is to commit the fallacy of reification. Individuals who say "I am gay" or "I am a lesbian" reify the connection between identity (an idea about the self) and a concrete behavior: "People become entrapped in a false consciousness of identifying themselves as *being* homosexual. They become boxed into their own biographies" (Sagarin 1973, 10). Of all the things people *do,* according to Sagarin, they choose to define themselves as *being* only one of those things. Reification is undesirable because it narrows the range of perceived options, identities, and roles available to individuals. It constricts the range of human experience and acts as a barrier to full self-actualization.

Sagarin is deeply concerned about the limitations that reification places on individual potential. He insists that people have many identities and that to define oneself in terms of any one is limiting. He states that men and women who label themselves as homosexual confuse who they are with what they sometimes do. They

> become entrapped or imprisoned in roles from which they could escape, or out of which they could develop. Their entrapment is due to a confusion of being with doing, and is facilitated by linguistic structures, particularly reifications (i.e., identity is a concept, an idea about the self). These reifications result in people believing they have an identity that is inescapable, and they then develop a set of rationalizations to support the identity and explanations for their failure to develop out of it. (Sagarin 1973, 154)

In a similar vein, Sagarin (1975) writes: "We speak of people being certain things when all we know is that they do certain things. The result is an imputed identity, or rather a special case of mistaken identity" (p. 25). According to Sagarin, then, men and women who define themselves as homosexual become trapped in a "false consciousness," victims of a "mistaken identity." In Chapter 6 I analyze this argument critically when I discuss the social-construction position toward homosexuality.

The Stability of Identities and Roles

From a social-role perspective, several voluntarily and involuntarily imposed factors explain the stability of homosexual identities and roles. Plummer (1975) lists ease, pleasure, and secondary gains as factors that individuals impose voluntarily upon themselves. Involuntarily imposed factors include problems of access, lack of "in-group" support, and public labeling as homosexual.

Voluntarily Imposed Factors

The ease of remaining committed to familiar patterns of behavior and the difficulties posed by adopting new lines of action encourage people to retain homosexual identities and roles. Once individuals become stabilized in homosexual roles, they may come to view the personal costs involved in taking on bisexual or heterosexual roles (e.g., time, energy, anxiety, and diminished sexual arousal) as outweighing the benefits of occupying a more conventional social status. Comfort and familiarity with homosexual identities and roles may crystallize the idea that it is "easier, more attractive, less costly to remain homosexual" (Plummer 1975, 50).

Individuals may also choose to retain their homosexual identities and roles because they are more pleasurable. Lesbians and gay males have learned that the "acts of falling, making, and being 'in love' with a member of the same sex can be both pleasurable and satisfying" (Plummer 1975, 151). Homosexual experience comes to be sought as an end in itself.

Secondary gains may also lead individuals to retain homosexual roles and identities. Clear advantages accrue to homosexual lifestyles. Lesbian and gay male sexuality is nonprocreative. Worries about pregnancy are nonexistent. Before the advent of the AIDS epidemic in the gay male community, recreational sex — within relationships or outside them — was possible at any time. (Sexual expression in the gay male community is now circumscribed by the "safe-sex" guidelines of avoiding an exchange of bodily fluids and anonymous sexual partners.) Homosexuals are also more tolerant of others labeled as "deviant," perhaps as a consequence of their own experience with stigma (Corbett, Troiden, and Dodder 1974). Greater social mobility and a higher standard of living (at least for gay males) have also been cited as advantages (Plummer 1975). Similar advantages, however, are open increasingly to heterosexual cohabitors and childless married couples.

Involuntarily Imposed Factors

Factors over which an individual has little or no control may also maintain the stability of homosexual roles and identities over time. One involuntarily imposed factor is the problem of access. As lesbians and gay males become older and more entrenched in homosexual experience, they become increasingly alienated from heterosexual experience, finding it

> difficult to make or maintain heterosexual contacts and increasingly disturbing to contemplate the idea of heterosexual activity. Earlier problems of access and identity may re-emerge in reverse if [they] should contemplate departure from the homosexual role: the secure world is now the "deviant" world, and the problematic world becomes the "straight" world. (Plummer 1975, 152)

A forty-year-old lesbian or gay male who has never dated or had a sexual experience with the opposite sex probably would be uncertain about how to initiate, enter, and maintain a heterosexual relationship, assuming that he or she was sexually responsive to the opposite sex. A new and different sexual script would have to be mastered. The perceived time, effort, and anxiety involved might well discourage such an individual from exploring this option.

The lack of in-group support is a second involuntarily imposed factor. Plummer (1975) contends that homosexuals who attempt to reenter the heterosexual world receive little or no support from homosexual friends and acquaintances. More often than not, those who try to "go straight" — that is, attempt to develop heterosexual or bisexual identities and roles — are ridiculed, not taken seriously, or rejected. A person's homosexual friends are likely to see his or her desires as unrealistic, self-deceptive, faddish, or a form of fence sitting. The individual is often accused of denying his or her "true" sexual and romantic nature.

Public labeling also fosters an involuntary commitment to the homosexual identity. Public labeling and denouncement as homosexual by official social-control agents, such as the police or courts, although relatively infrequent, may lead to role imprisonment: "To come before a court in a blaze of public scandal is to be publicly ushered into a deviant role, with very few chances of receiving official declarations of exit" (Plummer 1975, 152).

Conclusions

The social-role approach to homosexuality views homosexuality as a behavior or a social role and "the homosexual" as a social type, fabricated in a specific time and place. Homosexual behavior is acquired in the same fashion as other forms of conduct: through social learning. In terms of their sexual responsiveness and behaviors, people span a continuum from exclusive heterosexuality to exclusive homosexuality. Homosexuals and heterosexuals are more similar than different; they display differences of degree rather than kind.

From a social-role perspective, the homosexual identity is situation specific rather than transsituational; it is one of several important self-attributes rather than a form of subjective awareness underlying most social interactions. The social-role perspective emphasizes the presented dimension of homosexual identity; people are "homosexual" only in relation to social situations that permit homosexual identities to be announced and expressed through their corresponding roles. Outside the relevant situations, homosexual identities are latent or dormant. Situation-specific norms facilitate or prohibit the mobilization and expression of homosexual identities and roles. Considerably less attention is paid to the *experience* of homosexual identity: what the identity means to homosexuals themselves, how this self-identity is formed, and the role played by sexual preference in its formation.

In the social-role tradition, it is also argued that many people possess homosexual desires and engage in homosexual activities without ever self-defining as homosexual or adopting associated lifestyles. People commit the fallacy of reification when they narrowly equate their self-concept, a construct involving many situation-specific identities, with only one form of activity or behavior. Viewing oneself entirely or almost entirely in terms of a condition or a category of activity discourages experimentation with alternative lines of action and impedes self-actualization. The statement "I engage in homosexual behavior, therefore I am homosexual" is an example of reification.

Chapter 6   THE IDENTITY-CONSTRUCT APPROACH

The identity-construct (Plummer 1981b), or constructionist (Plummer 1981a, 1984), approach to homosexuality overlaps considerably with the social-role approach; the two resemble one another more than they differ. Both frameworks share the central idea that sexual conduct is primarily social in origin:

> Sexuality, for humans, is absolutely *unnatural*. For we are really quite removed from other species. They have little history to pass on from generation to generation; they have little language to communicate with; and they have little concern with moral or political issues. Our essential human nature, although biologically based, is one that is grounded upon diverse, historically changing cultures, and concomitantly, symbolism and language. (Plummer 1984, 222)

From both vantage points, questions of sexuality are cultural constructions, specific to time and place: what sexuality is, the purposes it serves, its manner of expression, and what it means to be sexual. Lesbianism and male homosexuality are similarly constructed and culture bound. Both perspectives also conceive of sexual behavior and responsiveness as spanning a spectrum from exclusive heterosexuality to exclusive homosexuality; the positions that people occupy on this spectrum result from social learning. In addition, the two outlooks share the idea that sexual identity is independent of sexual behavior.

The differences between the constructionist and social-role perspectives are primarily a matter of emphasis. The identity-construct paradigm is distinguished by its notion of what homosexual identity represents, its use of the term *homosexual,* its focus on the homosexual identity as a self-identity, and its emphasis on the centrality of homosexual identity.

What the Homosexual Identity Represents

As mentioned in Chapter 5, sociologist Edward Sagarin's (1973, 1975, 1976, 1979) position regarding homosexual identity represents the most extreme social-role stance. Sagarin developed and advanced the idea that the

80

homosexual identity is a "mistaken identity," a "confusion of being with doing." According to Sagarin, people are potentially responsive to both homosexual and heterosexual patterns. Thus there are no such persons as homosexuals or heterosexuals, but only individuals who engage in homosexual or heterosexual behavior. All people are homoerotic and heteroerotic to some degree, but not all individuals translate these yearnings into homosexual conduct; an even smaller number define themselves as homosexual, thereby falling victim to a form of "false consciousness."

A number of problems exist in Sagarin's argument that homosexual identities reflect a confusion of "being" with "doing." First, reifications are inevitable. Second, the lack of legitimacy accorded bisexual options is partly responsible for the reification of sexual identities. Third, perceptions of "being" (self-identity) may emerge in the absence of "doing" (activities). Fourth, problems of logical inconsistency and perspective undermine his argument. Fifth, self-identities thought to represent internal conditions (being) are perceived by social constructionists as more basic and central than those linked with roles (activities). Finally, as Lee Rainwater (1970) points out, reifications are inevitable because of the human need for consistency between activity and identity; behaviors become embedded in self-perceptions. I elaborate each of these criticisms of Sagarin's position in turn.

Few sociologists would deny the limitations that reifications place on self-actualization. Most interactionists, however, also argue that linguistic structures make reifications inevitable. People label themselves as "being" what they "do," especially when the "doing" involves dimensions of themselves that they have been socialized to view as essential. Individuals are likely to define themselves as homosexual if sexual and romantic impulses toward the same sex predominate; heterosexual if their erotic desires involve the opposite sex.

Any type of self-designation involves the "paradox of categorization" (Plummer 1981a). Labeling the self in terms of desires or activities provides structure: it identifies and locates the self as a specific type of social object. Placing the self in one social category, however, excludes it simultaneously from other categories and imposes limits on the self:

> On the one hand, labels are useful devices — they give order to chaos, structure to openness, security to confusion. Knowing that one is gay is much more comforting than living with the precariousness of confused sexual identities. On the other hand, labels are destructive devices — they restrict where other choices are possible, they control and limit possible variety, they narrow human experimentation. (Plummer 1981a, 108)

People define themselves sexually as homosexual or heterosexual for reasons that range well beyond a confusion of being with doing. These reasons include the direction and type of their sexual and romantic experiences, and their reactions to these experiences; the cultural view of sexual preferences as deeply rooted and resistant to change; and social pressure on adults to adopt either heterosexual or homosexual lifestyles. The lack of recognition granted to bisexuality is an especially potent reason why many people define themselves as either homosexual or heterosexual.

In principle, three sexual orientations and associated identities are available: homosexual, bisexual (ambisexual), or heterosexual. Sexual identity is a perception of self in relation to sexual or romantic settings; this image usually is linked to self-perceived sexual orientation.

In the United States, however, sexual orientations and sexual identities are polarized or dichotomized. People are socialized to see themselves as either heterosexual or homosexual. The cultural view of sexual preference as dichotomous has, in part, prevented the bisexual option from becoming institutionalized—established as a recognized sexual pattern. The public at large, regardless of sexual orientation, views bisexuality as inauthentic, a cop-out, a form of fence sitting (Blumstein and Schwartz 1974, 1977; Humphreys 1979; Paul 1983/1984, 1985; Ponse 1978; Warren 1974; Zinik 1985). In popular culture, bisexuals are believed to have clear-cut preferences for either heterosexual or homosexual patterns, and "really" to belong to the more preferred pattern.

The unwillingness of people in general, and significant others in particular, to acknowledge bisexual preferences makes it more difficult to maintain and validate these preferences than heterosexual identities, which are supported continuously by sociocultural institutions, or homosexual identities, which are recognized and reinforced by institutional arrangements within the homosexual community.

The widespread lack of social support for bisexual identities is compounded by the issue of competing loyalties. Bisexual individuals must cultivate sociosexual relationships with members of both sexes. Concurrent intimate relationships with both sexes, however, may generate a host of problems (Brownfain 1985; Coleman 1985a, 1985b; Wolf 1985). If an individual's intimate partners know about his or her bisexual interests, they may feel threatened and demand that he or she choose one path over the other. Not informing partners of dual sexual interests also creates problems: The perceived need to perform as heterosexual (or homosexual) and to keep same-sex (or opposite-sex) involvements secret may produce tension and guilt that strain the relationship severely. The lack of public affirmation for bisexual identities and lifestyles and the issue of competing loyalties lead many bisexuals to conclude that the emotional costs of a bisexual lifestyle outweigh the benefits; it is easier and less costly to channel their energies into exclusively heterosexual or homosexual patterns.

Research cited in Chapters 1 and 2 also undermines Sagarin's argument that homosexual identity represents a confusion of being with doing. Some people in certain contexts define themselves as homosexual even in the absence of homosexual activity (Blumstein and Schwartz 1974; Faderman 1984/1985; Lessard 1972; Lockard 1985; Ponse 1978; Ross 1971). In these cases they did not confuse "being" with "doing."

If homosexuality and heterosexuality were simply matters of behavior, one might wonder why homosexuals do not confuse their "being" with their heterosexual "doing." As indicated in Chapter 4, most committed homosexuals have had heterosexual experiences, but still formed homosexual self-identities. Experience taught them that homosexual roles expressed their sexual and emotional needs more validly than heterosexual roles, which produced dissonance:

> Overcoming all the social barriers erected in their path, they find the gay identity a more valid expression of the human condition than that afforded by a heterosexual one. For them, the "tyranny of isness" is less appalling than the tyranny of isn'tness. (Humphreys 1979, 241)

(The "tyranny of isness" refers to the belief that one "is" what one "does.")

Homosexuality and heterosexuality consist of more than social roles; they also include sexual orientations or preferences. Exclusive homosexuals who attempt to change their sexual preferences from homosexual to heterosexual meet with failure (Humphreys 1979). Only highly motivated people with bisexual histories and fantasies can be taught (conditioned) to respond sexually to the opposite sex (Masters and Johnson 1979), but their erotic interest in the same sex remains unextinguished.

Sagarin's argument that homosexual identities represent a confusion of being with doing is also plagued by problems of logical inconsistency and perspective—tacit assumptions about the "goodness" or "badness" of homosexuality. Although Sagarin goes to great lengths, for example, to show that homosexual identities thwart self-actualization by constricting the scope of available sexual options, he mentions only in passing that heterosexual identities are reified similarly. Nor does Sagarin acknowledge that the process of identity entrapment cuts both ways; heterosexual identities are imposed on people with or without their consent. Along these lines, Humphreys (1979) has argued that "all the accouterments of our society reinforce a heterosexual identity and individuals who do not claim a homosexual one are entrapped in a heterosexual identity by *default*" (p. 240).

Sagarin further displays his essentially hostile view of homosexuality in the terms he uses to describe homosexual identity. The assertion that homosexual identity is spawned by "false consciousness," for example, raises the question, "False from whose point of view?" Because Sagarin accepts conventional wisdom at face value and sees homosexuality as undesirable, it is not surprising that he describes homosexual identity as inauthentic. (He does not, however, label perceptions of "being" tied to heterosexual "doing" as "false consciousness.") Yet from an "insider's" perspective, that of homosexuals themselves, the homosexual identity is regarded quite differently, as representing authentic feelings and valid needs.

In a similar vein, Sagarin adopts the perspective of the wider, stigmatizing society ("Public Perceptions of Gays" 1982) when he describes the homosexual identity as a "negative status" without qualifying the term. His claim is generally accurate; few societies have condemned homosexuality as savagely as the United States. Sagarin fails to point out, however, that the dominant perspective is not the only possible view of homosexuality. From the vantage point of many homosexuals, the homosexual status is neither negative nor disvalued. Depending on perspective, the homosexual identity may be a burden or a blessing.

Sagarin also shows his negative bias when he equates homosexuality with a failure to develop. Homosexuals, he states, believe "they have an identity that is inescapable" and invent a set of "rationalizations for their failure to develop out of it" (Sagarin 1975, 154). His "developmental failure" argument reflects nothing more than unsupported professional opinion, a judgment at odds with the empirical evidence. Moreover, he makes no mention of an analogous developmental failure on the part of heterosexuals. If homosexuals are unable to make the transition to heterosexuality, heterosexuals are similarly crippled by an inability to make the transition to homosexuality. The sexual experiences of exclusive heterosexuals are as narrow and self-limiting as the sexual activities of exclusive homosexuals; the two groups differ only in the gender of the persons who attract them sexually.

Criticism may also be leveled against Sagarin's (1979) challenge that homosexual women and men must either acknowledge that they did not choose their homosexual identities freely or explain why they abandoned the advantages of heterosexual lifestyles:

> Deviants are faced with a dilemma of their own making. If they claim that the feelings arouse spontaneously and are beyond their control, they then relinquish any semblance of free choice, admit to being captive of an unconsciousness that may or may not be to their liking, and their defenses of identity become *ex*

post facto justifications. If they claim that the feelings are those that they would wish to have and would have chosen had there been a free choice, they must take responsibility for and explain the rationale of making a choice contrary to the advantages offered by an alternate path. (p. 11)

Sagarin places homosexuals (and heterosexuals) in a no-win situation.

People do not choose their sexual feelings (or any other feelings, for that matter). They do choose to act — or not to act — on their erotic impulses. To make sense of their own and others' sexualities, individuals draw upon systems of meaning contained within the sexual scenarios of the wider culture. The accounts they offer to explain and justify their sexual preferences, identities, and actions are, at rock bottom, rationalizations manufactured and legitimized by existing sociocultural arrangements at particular historical points and contexts. Sagarin's conceptualization of homosexual identity is influenced by his assumptions about the nature of homosexuality and homosexuals. His position is anchored in a conventional wisdom that paints a hostile and unflattering picture of sexually variant persons.

Sagarin's (1975) analogy between tennis play and homosexual behavior reveals another weakness of his argument that homosexual identity represents a confusion of being with doing:

You were not a tennis player until you started to play tennis, and nothing forced you to choose that path. At any time, you can stop playing tennis, and you will not be a tennis player, you will be an ex-player. You can give it up because you have other interests. You should start thinking of people as homosexuals the way people are tennis players. It is something they do, not something they are. (p. 151)

At first blush, this argument appears to make a great deal of sense: Both playing tennis and homosexual relations are behaviors, and each activity is capable of generating a self-identity, such as "I am a tennis player" and "I am a homosexual," that is elicited by relevant situations (Humphreys 1979).

The descriptive value of the analogy is negated by several problems. First, most people do not usually see sports activities as mirroring basic, essential needs, unless the activities are occupational. Second, the wider society is far less likely to stigmatize sports activities than homosexual activities. Third, sports activities generally need not be disguised, underplayed, or denied, but these maneuvers are commonly associated with homosexual interests and activities. Fourth, sports identities (even occupational ones) usually are not seen as permanent; it is possible to be an ex-football player, for example, whereas sexual identities usually are regarded as resistant to change. It is unlikely that sexually inactive adults, for example, would label themselves as "ex-homosexuals" or "ex-heterosexuals" (Humphreys 1979). Fifth, self-identities vary in their centrality; some are more basic than others. Self-identifications involving race, biological sex, gender identity ("masculine" or "feminine" perceptions of self), occupation, and sexual preference are constructed conventionally as representing essences or basic dimensions of self rather than avocational interests, such as tennis.

For constructionists, social roles (behavior) are not the only sources of self-identity. Group ties, such as religion and race, also may provide a basis for self-identity. So, too, may internal conditions or qualities. Katz (1972) defines an *essence* as an internal quality thought to be "reflected" or "represented" by conduct, but not necessarily present in the conduct itself. Building upon Katz, Ponse (1978) uses the term *essential identity* to denote identities perceived as "going beyond an embodiment of mere roles or attributes, referring to the state of *being* of the individual rather than the mere doing of an individual" (p. 6). Biological sex, gender, intelligence, or sexual preference, for example, are inner conditions that generate self-identity. In the context of lesbianism, Richardson (1981b) has written:

> It is also important to recognize that the predominance of a belief in the essentiality of a lesbian identity has been significant not merely at the level of how mainstream society has perceived and reacted towards lesbianism, but also in the meanings ascribed to such an identification by lesbians themselves. Many homosexual women do define lesbianism as an immutable characteristic of their personality, and it is a core-construct of their self. (p. 117)

In Chapter 4 I showed that many committed homosexuals, at some point in their lives, regard their homosexual identities as essential identities (Faderman 1983/1984; Lockard 1985; Plummer 1981a, 1981b; Ponse 1978; Richardson 1981b; Troiden 1977, 1979, 1983/1984; Warren 1974; Warren and Ponse 1977).

Finally, the view that homosexual self-identification represents a confusion of being with doing ignores the human need for consistency between identity and activity. People see themselves in terms of their activities and feelings. Sociologist Lee Rainwater (1970) maintains that "the need for a valid identity is fundamental; everybody needs to be somebody" (p. 374). Rainwater argues that an identity is valid when individuals perceive a congruence between three elements: who they feel they are, who they proclaim themselves to be, and where they feel their society places them.

People obtain the tools necessary for constructing valid identities from their cultures:

> Individuals are led to announce a particular identity when they feel it is congruent with their needs, and the society influences these needs by its willingness to validate such announcements by a congruent placement. As individuals seek to build identities valid in terms of their own needs, they use the resources — the values, norms, and social techniques — which their culture makes available to them. Each individual tries on identities that emerge from the cultural material available to him and tests them by making appropriate announcements. If these announcements meet with success, he will maintain his identity until it is no longer congruent with his inner promptings. (Rainwater, 1970, 374)

In Chapters 2 and 4 I described the difficulty that people experience in learning to affix meanings to their feelings and in sorting out what emotions mean, especially when the activities thought to represent them are socially condemned and disvalued.

The stigma borne by homosexuals, and the typically negative imagery used to describe them and their lifestyles, discourages people from interpreting and defining their feelings as homoerotic. Few tasks would seem more difficult than assuming membership in a social category infused with public opprobrium. A denial of needs, however, may generate identity loss or confusion:

> One of the deepest anxieties human beings can experience is that which comes from the loss of a sense of identity. Such a loss comes about either when there is a disjunction between the self being announced and the needs pressing for gratification or when the announced identity is not validated by others. In either case, the identity becomes invalid for the individual once he recognizes the state of affairs. For a time he may not do so, resisting recognition with intrapsychic mechanisms in defense against internal invalidation or by self-delusion about social invalidation. (Rainwater 1970, 375-76)

As I indicated in Chapter 4, many committed homosexuals experienced their sexual identities as invalid during adolescence. They perceived neither heterosexual or homosexual identities as genuinely expressing their emerging sexual and romantic needs. Perceptions of themselves as heterosexual were at variance with their homosexual desires, but the lack of social validation for homosexual identities, combined with ignorance about homosexuals and homosexuality, hindered the formation of their homosexual self-identities.

In the homosexual context, the experience of valid identity entails more than acknowledging and acting upon sexual desires. Individuals must also gain access to audiences that look upon homosexual feelings, behaviors, and identities as valid expressions of the human condition, and treat them as such. For committed homosexuals, the homosexual satellite culture fills this role by providing a range of settings where people may feel that they are homosexual, present themselves as homosexual, and know that they are viewed as such by others. The experience of invalid identity, in contrast, occurs in contexts that do not permit homosexual identities and roles to be announced and expressed. In these cases, however, it is not the homosexual identity that is perceived as invalid, but the situationally imposed heterosexual identity.

Despite its usefulness, Rainwater's conceptualization of valid identity has a few weaknesses. First, Rainwater does not define the concept of valid identity as much as he outlines elements necessary for the realization of identity. He describes the experience of valid identity rather than defining the concept. Second, he uses the term *identity* as if people possess only one. As I argued in Chapter 3, it makes more sense to describe people as possessing one self-concept and many identities, only a few of which are mobilized or manifested in any given situation. Third, the idea that people possess one self-concept and a number of situationally mobilized identities explains research that has revealed inconsistencies between general attitudes and situation-specific behavior (Anjzen and Fishbein 1973).

Use of the Term Homosexual

Identity-construct and social-role theorists attribute different meanings to the term homosexual . Whereas social-role theorists use the word as an adjective to denote sexual behavior, feelings, or fantasies involving the same sex, identity-construct theorists use the word connotatively. While they agree that homosexuality is theoretically an experience or a form of behavior, they point out that in practice, common usage has expanded the meanings of the word to encompass inner conditions or states of mind:

> Roughly since the start of this century many people have come to use the term as a noun: "the homosexual" refers to a type, a species, a form of being. Mere experience is transformed into core being — the description becomes the thing. (Plummer 1981a, 94)

According to constructionists, cultural scenarios in the West socialize people to believe that heterosexuality and homosexuality are essences, although they are not. Because homosexuality is *constructed* as an essence, it is *experienced* as an essence. Homosexuality becomes a form of being only when it has been defined as such:

> Thus, however inadequate the term "the homosexual," or "the gay" may be to social scientists, it does exist as a construct in the wider world that many people can opt to identify with. In so doing many people come to read their past as symptomatic of a "real gayness" that was there all along. (Plummer 1981a, 95-96)

Identity-construct theorists, then, use *homosexual* as a noun to capture the sociocultural reality of homosexuality, rather than the essential reality. From a constructionist viewpoint, however, the self-induced act of "essentializing" sexual identity is "restricting and controlling" (Plummer 1981a) but inevitable, given the paradox of categorization.

The Homosexual Identity as Self-Identity

As I indicated in Chapter 3, the homosexual identity may be a self-identity, a perceived identity, or a presented identity, depending on context. In Chapter 5 I discussed the emphasis that the social-role school places on the presented dimension of homosexual identity. By contrast, identity-construct study has focused on the homosexual identity as a self-identity, incorporating insiders' perspectives into their definitions of identity. The formation of homosexual self-identities (as described in Chapter 4, for example) is one issue that has commanded constructionist attention. Another such issue is the subjective *experience* of homosexual identity.

Carol Warren's (1972, 1974) pioneering study of identity in the gay male community was one of the first to document the perspective of male homosexuals toward their sexual identities. She concluded that the way gay males view homosexuality and gayness is more complex than the way heterosexuals view it; different criteria are used, and subtler distinctions are made, to determine who is or is not homosexual and to differentiate components of gay identity.

From the perspective of gay males, the fusion of same-sex emotionality and sexuality into a "meaningful whole" is the hallmark of genuine homosexuality. Same-sex love relationships, rather than homosexual activities, distinguish homosexuals from nonhomosexuals:

> The romantic-sexual act fusion serves as a highly significant benchmark symbol of converted self-identity for many members [of the gay community] who indicate that [the linking] of romantic-sex acts differentiates the "true" homosexual from the one who is simply experimenting. (Warren 1972, 223)

The components of gay identity are equally intricate and subtle:

> A *homosexual identity* is distinguished from a gay identity by the gay community, although not by the stigmatizing society. A homosexual identity simply describes one's sexual orientation, whereas a gay identity implies affiliation with the gay community in a cultural and sociable sense. A homosexual, for the community, is one who both practices homosexuality and admits it, whereas a gay person is someone who does all that and also identifies and interacts with the gay world. (Warren 1974, 149-50)

In keeping with Warren's informants, then, a *homosexual identity* describes a kind of sexual behavior, sexual preference, and sexual identity. *Gay identity,* in contrast, encompasses not only the dimensions of homosexual identity but also social involvement in the homosexual community and same-sex romantic (emotional) attachments. Warren admits that this distinction is somewhat forced; it was made only when she, or the circumstances, demanded it.

Chesebro's (1981) constructionist conceptualization of the term *gay* also is etched against the backdrop of the gay community:

> The word gay is thus a summative or constitutional concept. It is multidimensional in the sense that a world view, self-conception, group membership, lifestyle, and affectional and sexual preferences—as well as one's sense of pride and power—are adopted in an actual, implied, or potentially confrontational context. (p. 187)

Strictly speaking, Warren's and Chesebro's definitions of identity are conceptually unclear. Identity is a cognitive concept: an idea about the self, not a behavior. Both conceptualizations merge behavior and cognitions within an ideational construct, which contributes to conceptual fuzziness. On the other hand, the conceptual status of identity is separate from its self-perceived or experiential status. The *experience* of identity differs from what identity *is* conceptually. Although conceptually unclear, Warren's and

Chesebro's definitions of homosexual identity convey accurately the experience of homosexual identity at specific points in its formation.

Warren concludes her analysis by arguing that stigma, more than anything else, affects the *experience* of gay identity:

> There are certain generalities that describe the experience of being gay. Perhaps the most important elements are totality, belonging, and distinction. *Totality.* The gay world, because it is stigmatized and set apart, is one that demands total identification. *Belonging.* With the experience of totality comes the sense of belonging to and with those who are the same. *Distinction.* Belonging involves distinction. Above all, gay identity is distinct. It sets the experience of being gay apart from the experience of life in mass society. (Warren 1974, 162-64)

Totality, belonging, and distinction, however, may describe most accurately the experience of homosexual identity near the time of self-definition as homosexual, when the identity is still novel and not yet taken for granted. As I indicated in Chapter 4, the centrality and significance of homosexual identities appear to wax and wane.

When Ponse (1978, 1984) examined the meanings that lesbians attach to their homosexual identities and experiences, she obtained results similar to Warren's. The women she studied viewed lesbianism as involving more than a role or behavior. Women actively involved in the lesbian community constructed and experienced their sexual and romantic feelings, lifestyles, and self-identities as essences, fundamental conditions distinguishing them from heterosexuals:

> Most of these women consider "lesbian" as referring to a state of being rather than as descriptive of behavior. Lesbian identity here then is construed in terms of an ongoing, pervasive and immutable aspect of self, as contrasted with being descriptive of situated behavior or mere sexual activity. Being a lesbian according to most of these women is far more inclusive of lifestyle and orientation than simple activity. The notion of gayness as a pervasive quality of the self, informing the total person and definitive of a lifestyle is most celebrated in the activist sector of the lesbian community. Many activist women view gayness as pervading nonsexual aspects of the self as well. (Ponse 1984, 26-27)

Like Warren, Ponse argues that stigma and secrecy highlight and amplify the centrality of homosexual identities.

Explaining the Centrality of Identity

Another difference between the identity-construct and social-role models is the emphasis of the former on explaining the centrality of homosexual identities among lesbians and gay males. At least three factors explain the self-perceived salience of homosexual identities: (1) institutionalized social-structural patterns of domination and subordination that "inferiorize" homosexuality; (2) stigma and secrecy; and (3) the nature of identity transformations themselves.

Domination and Subordination

According to Barry Adam (1978a), the social-structural relationships between heterosexual and homosexual groups are framed by patterns of domination and subordination. Dominant groups produce and maintain social order because they control the bulk of the socially valued resources. Control over resources enables these groups to create and control social institutions, which are structured to maximize the life chances of dominant groups by minimizing those of subordinate groups. Dominant groups survive at the expense of subordinate groups through institutional arrangements that systematically "inferiorize" subordinate groups. *Inferiorization,* then, refers to the creation of social inequality.

The inferiorization of homosexuals is evident at all levels of society and in all major institutions. Dominant institutions inferiorize subordinate groups by constructing the characteristics that allegedly set them apart (e.g., effeminacy, same-sex attraction) and that justify their exclusion from the hierarchy of access. Institutions of social control—the police and the courts, for example—assume attitudes of official blindness and neglect toward acts of aggression leveled against inferiorized groups (e.g., gay bashing) and "at the same time, the inferiorized themselves are more frequently subject to arrest, police harassment, and conviction by courts" (Adam 1978a, 28). In the case of homosexuals, the mode of sexual expression itself has been criminalized.

Legal institutions condone inferiorization explicitly by defending the constitutionality of discriminatory practices (e.g., state sodomy statutes); they routinize inferiorization implicitly by not outlawing discrimination in employment and place of residence on the basis of sexual preference.

Economic institutions maintain inferiorization through discriminatory hiring and by barring homosexuals from certain occupations (e.g., the clergy, national security), trade unions (e.g., firefighters), and voluntary associations (e.g., Big Brothers). Political institutions also remain, for the most part, "the monopoly of noninferiorized people."

Institutions that transmit culture—schools, churches, the publishing industry, and the mass media—define the personal and social characteristics of inferiorized people:

> The systematic selection of attributes of inferiorized peoples for public presentation constructs an image which rationalizes inferiorized status for both privileged and inferiorized groups. Inferiorized people discover their "objective" identity lives beyond their control; the image of self, institutionalized by cultural agents, exists alien to their own experience and self-expression. (Adam 1978a, 30-31)

Inferiorized people tend to be described (if acknowledged at all) in disrespectable contexts: crime, physical disease, immorality, mental illness. Homosexuals, for example, have been variously portrayed as child molesters, mentally ill, and sinful.

Medical institutions also contribute to inferiorization by presenting the life patterns of inferiorized people as unnatural ("Heterosexuality is assumed to be the biological norm"), as reflecting disease ("Homosexuality is caused by pathological fears of the opposite sex"), as invalid or inauthentic ("You don't really find homosexual relations satisfying, you're just experiencing confusion about what you really need"). The maintenance of the social order, as currently constituted, depends on the continuing inferiorization of lesbians and gay men. The general practice of inferiorization and the more specific pattern of stigma shape the experience and the life chances of homosexuals.

Stigma and Secrecy

Sociologist Erving Goffman (1963) uses the term stigma to describe a socially disvalued behavior, attribute, or condition that disqualifies the possessor from full social acceptance. A stigma "marks" or "brands" the individual as different, setting him or her apart from "normals"—people who do not vary significantly from the particular expectations under consideration. Jones et al. (1984) use the more neutral term *mark* to describe socially discrediting attributes.

Goffman identifies three kinds of stigma: *abominations of the body, blemishes of individual character,* and *tribal stigmas.* Abominations of the body are disfiguring physical conditions that serve as barriers to full social acceptance, such as being blind, crippled, deaf, or mute. Blemishes of individual character refer to undesirable conditions that are not immediately apparent, but are grounds for discrimination only if discovered. Potentially stigmatized people can hide their stigmas and may pose as "normal" among conventionals. Homosexuals, prostitutes, strippers, liars, and drug addicts are examples. Tribal stigmas are acquired by virtue of lineage or group ties. In the United States, national origin, race, or religion traditionally have served as bases for unequal social treatment.

Goffman and Jones et al. both note that stigmas may be apparent or hidden. If stigmas are immediately apparent, the stigmatized individuals are *discredited* (Goffman 1963). People with hidden stigmas, by contrast, are socially *discreditable*—recipients of bad treatment only if found out (Goffman 1963). Jones et al. (1984) use the terms *marked* and *markable* in drawing similar distinctions. As shown in Chapter 4, most homosexuals are markable rather than marked, because they choose not to disclose their homosexuality to most social audiences.

Jones et al. (1984) have isolated six dimensions along which stigmas may vary: *concealability, course, disruptiveness, aesthetic qualities, origin, and peril.* Concealability is the degree to which the stigma is hidden, obvious, or controllable—that is, may be disguised. Course is the ultimate outcome of the stigma: whether the pattern or condition is changeable or permanent. Disruptiveness is the degree to which the stigma impedes or "blocks" communication and interaction. Aesthetic qualities are the extent to which the stigma makes the owner appear "repellent, ugly or upsetting." Origin refers to the condition(s) thought to cause the mark and to the degree of self-responsibility or other responsibility: Is the mark voluntary or involuntary? Peril addresses the danger posed by the stigma, including its seriousness and imminence.

Forsyth and Gramling (1986) elaborate two additional dimensions of stigma: *exploitation* and *historical precedent.* Exploitation is the extent to which unmarked persons use the marked "to obtain goods, services, or considerations not ordinarily available to unmarked persons in similar circumstances" (p. 49). Historical precedent refers to the fact that "the way a particular mark will be viewed is largely a product of how it has been viewed in the past, and the extent of mythology which has collected around it" (p. 50).

Stigma shapes powerfully both the formation and the experience of homosexual identity. As I noted in Chapter 4, stigma affects homosexual identity formation by creating problems of guilt, secrecy, access, and identity:

> To apprehend that your diversity is taboo is to exist either in public shame or private guilt. Stigma creates silence, ban breeds solitariness. The struggle here is to find the right words to use and the right person to approach. A final problem centers upon identity. Once any anomaly in gender or sexual experience is

sensed, questions will be posed about identity. The struggle is
on to find out who one really is. (Plummer 1984, 236-37)

Stigma affects gay and lesbian experiences of homosexual identity
because homosexuals are markable along all eight dimensions. As I indicated in Chapter 4, most homosexuals *conceal* their homosexuality from
at least some social audiences. The need for secrecy saturates homosexual
identity with significance:

> The perceived need to maintain secrecy tends to promote com-
> mitment to the gay world as a place where the gay self can be
> validated and accepted. At the same time, the care that must be
> taken in interaction with heterosexuals to obscure the gay self,
> renders the individual particularly alive to the gay self and the
> gay world. The gay self becomes salient precisely because it
> must be hidden. It is reiterated and reinforced in inner con-
> sciousness. The gay world is invoked within the walls of the self
> as a support and sanctuary. (Ponse 1980, 159)

As I noted in Chapter 5, homosexuality has been constructed socially as an
immutable, *permanent* condition, which implicates the *course* of stigma.
To some people, openly lesbian and gay individuals are *disruptive,* trying to
impose their homosexual lifestyles on others. Some heterosexuals find
stereotypically "homosexual" lesbians or gay males, or those who display
love and affection in public, *aesthetically displeasing.* Because some people
see homosexuality as a matter of choice, they hold homosexuals responsible
for the *origin* of their stigmatized condition.

The alleged *peril* of homosexuality is another component of stigma
that has long captivated the popular imagination. In the United States,
homosexuals have been portrayed as sinners, as child molesters, as mentally
ill, as security risks, and (more recently) as AIDS threats. Homosexuals are
also *exploitable.* Homophobia — an irrational fear and hatred of homosexuals — has been used by politicians, such as Senator Joseph McCarthy, and
by religious leaders, such as the Reverend Jerry Falwell, to promote right-
wing political agendas. Finally, in 1986, the Supreme Court of the United
States used the eighth component of stigma, *historical precedent,* to uphold
the constitutionality of state sodomy statutes.

Self-defined homosexuals respond to stigma by using the stigma-
management strategies discussed in Chapter 4. They may try to evade
stigma through denial, repair, capitulation, avoidance, redefinition (or
neutralization), passing, or group alignment. They may confront stigma
covertly through blending (avoidance without hiding) or covering, or overtly

through minstrelization, or conversion. Ponse's (1978, 100) term "challenges to the heterosexual order" is similar to conversion.

As I indicated in Chapter 4, passing is the most common stigma-evasion strategy. In order to pass successfully, however, undeclared homosexuals must attend to aspects of everyday interactions that others treat as unthinking routines. Warren's (1974) and Ponse's (1978) informants who passed commonly reported monitoring their gestures, speech patterns, inflections, eye contact with others, appearances, and personal revelations to avoid doing anything deemed homosexual.

To the extent that individuals are genuinely successful at passing, they experience the pain of learning what more conventional people really think about their sort of people. Undeclared homosexuals are *mundanely stigmatized* (Warren and Johnson 1972). They are exposed routinely to negative characterizations of homosexuality in the mass media, derogatory jokes about "queers," and the undisguised homophobia of co-workers. Mundane stigmatization informs hidden homosexuals graphically of their socially marginal status. Successful passing, however, demands that lesbians and gay males remain neutral in the face of detrimental remarks about homosexual people.

Passing may assume one of three forms: *counterfeit secrecy, restriction, and segregation.* Counterfeit secrecy involves structuring friend and family relationships so they are "patterned by the tacit negotiation of mutual pretense in which the gay self is not acknowledged" (Ponse 1980, 165). All parties agree implicitly not to focus on issues of sexuality and sexual identity. In instances of restriction, personal interactions are limited to homosexuals; nonhomosexual relationships are avoided (Ponse 1978). Segregation involves separating social worlds into homosexual and heterosexual spheres and hoping that the two never collide (Ponse 1978).

The stigma attached to homosexuality and the perceived need to mask homosexual identities and lifestyles infuse homosexual identities with a significance and centrality they would not possess otherwise. Stigma affects what homosexuals are willing to disclose about themselves, with whom they are open, with whom they associate, and how they feel about themselves. The centrality of the homosexual identity may dominate or dwarf other self-identities in a person's consciousness until (as was shown in Chapter 4) he or she can arrive at some sort of accommodation between sexual identity and social environment.

Identity Change

In addition to inferiorization, stigma and secrecy, the nature of identity change partly explains the significance that lesbians and gay males attach to their homosexual identities.

From the perspective of symbolic interactionism, adult identity transformations may be regarded as occupying a place on a continuum. On one end are the easily accomplished *alternations*. Alternations involve taking on identities that are *prescribed* (positively sanctioned) or at least permitted within the perspectives of the groups to which an individual belongs. These groups value the new identity and see it as appropriate. In discussing alternations, Travisano (1970) notes:

> One joins a conservation club or perhaps frequents a different bar. Little change is noticed by most of the person's others. There is no trauma. There is little reflection on the part of the actor either before or after. There is not an important change in universes of discourse. (p. 601)

On the other end of the continuum are radical *conversions,* unsettling and massive adult identity transformations. Conversions involve transitions to identities that are *proscribed* (forbidden) within an individual's established reference groups and that negate or invalidate a formerly established identity. In other words, conversions occur when people adopt identities forbidden by the groups to which they belonged formerly. In addition, old group ties are replaced by new groups that support the new identity.

The ideal-typical conversion may be regarded as involving a negative identity (from the vantage point of the "old" groups) that pervades all interactions. Again, to quote Travisano (1970):

> The person goes through a period of intense "inner struggle." The actor reflects at great length on the change. The actor and all his others see his change as monumental and he is identified by himself and others as a new or different person. The actor has a new universe of discourse which negates the values and meanings of his old ones by exposing the "fallacies" of their assumptions and reasoning. The actor has great involvement with his new identity. (p. 601)

The hallmarks of a conversion are confusion and inner struggle before conversion; the adoption of identities that are proscribed or forbidden; a perception by the actor that the identity change is monumental and that the new identity is central to most interactions; a switch in allegiance from one group perspective to another; a reorganization of life; and a change in symbolic world.

Self-definition as homosexual may be looked upon as constituting an identity conversion for a number of reasons. First, as I noted in Chapter 4, lesbians and gay males typically experience considerable confusion and inner turmoil about the nature and meanings of their sexual feelings before they label themselves as homosexual. Second, the decision to define themselves as homosexual and adopt corresponding lifestyles is to become involved with an identity and way of life that is forbidden or proscribed within the frameworks of their established groups (e.g., family, church or synagogue, schools).

Third, the social, affectional, and sexual changes involved in the transition to homosexual status are viewed by both self and others (if they learn of it) as monumental, and the new identity as central to most, if not all, interactions. Stigma and secrecy infuse homosexual identities with an awareness of public opprobrium; the homosexual identity becomes pervasive.

Fourth, self-definition as homosexual involves a switch in allegiance. The decision to adopt a positive, "insider's" portrayal of homosexuality ("gay is good," "gay and proud") entails a simultaneous rejection of the "outsider's" or conventional image of homosexuality as "sinful," "sick," or "unnatural."

Fifth, when lesbians and gay males have defined themselves as homosexual, they are faced with a number of dilemmas whose resolution involves a reorganization of their lives. They must consider, for example, the advisability of leading "double lives." They must consider concealing their homosexual preferences from family, friends, and colleagues or disclosing their homosexual identities to some, most, or all nonhomosexual audiences; of becoming involved socially in the homosexual subculture or limiting their involvement in the community; of entering into a marriage-type relationship with a member of the same sex, remaining single, or cultivating both heterosexual and homosexual relationships; of living with a lover as a couple or maintaining separate residences; of changing jobs or geographical locales in order to work and live in an atmosphere more supportive of homosexual identities and lifestyles or staying put and keeping the worlds of work and intimacy somewhat or strictly separated.

Sixth, a genuine conversion, according to Travisano, always entails a change in people's symbolic worlds; a quite distinctive perception of the world emerges in the wake of a conversion. With respect to male homosexuals, Plummer (1975) notes:

> To put it simply: male homosexuals are "boy" watchers. Such a pivotal distinction means of course that people in the homosexual subculture regularly and routinely apprehend other men as erotic objects: at work, watching television, walking around the street, at parties, in moments of "time out" and reverie, the young man's fancy turns to other men. It is the world of the waking heterosexual man in reverse—with all the variations in

kinds of objects and intensity of attraction that this implies. (p. 159)

The same could be said for lesbians.

Because a person's fundamental way of looking at the world is altered in the wake of conversion, reversions to earlier frames of reference, identity, and lifestyle are rare. Anselm Strauss (1969) writes:

> One misconception about conversion is that when a person becomes *partly* converted, and then is "lost," he returns to his previous identity. This is probably not so, for once a man has absorbed a new vocabulary with which to name and perceive the world, including his own actions, he can scarcely tear the vocabulary out of his brain. (p. 123; italics added)

What is true for the "partly" converted is even more true for the totally converted. In instances of total conversion, when people adopt universes of discourse antithetical to those held previously, genuine reversions to older group perspectives are exceedingly difficult and rare.

Conclusions

Constructionist analysis focuses on the homosexual identity as a self-identity, and the experience and formation of homosexual identities are of particular interest to identity-construct theorists. In addition, an appreciation of the subjective experience of identity has led constructionists to incorporate insiders' perceptions into their definitions of identity. Although they acknowledge that in principle the term *homosexual* refers to behavior, constructionists prefer to use the term as a noun to capture the sociocultural reality of homosexuality as a constructed essence. Structurally ingrained patterns of inferiorization, stigma and secrecy, and the dynamics of identity conversion explain the significance and centrality of homosexual identities.

The passage of time, experience, and changes in life situation, however, bring changes in interpretations of converted identities; the value, significance, centrality, and permanence attributed to these identities are not static, but are modified by experience. Homosexuals may see their homosexual identity, for example, as dwarfing or dominating their other identities in the wake of defining themselves as homosexual, but this centrality may recede over time as other identities and roles demand allegiance.

My own approach to homosexual identity is a synthesis of the social-role and the identity-construct perspectives. From the perspective of social-role theory, a homosexual identity is a perception of self as homosexual in relation to sexual and romantic contexts. Homosexual identity, in principle, is no more or less central than other important identities, such as age, gender, race, and occupation. Like other important identities, homosexual perceptions of self are mobilized and manifested in situations that permit them to be expressed through behavior; otherwise, they remain latent, or unexpressed. The experience of homosexual identity may occur if homosexual elements are introduced into the situation.

I agree with identity-construct theorists that the practice of inferiorization, sociocultural traditions that "essentialize" sexual preferences, and stigma and secrecy infuse homosexual identity with a significance it would not possess otherwise:

> On one level to love someone of the same sex is remarkably inconsequential — after all, but for some anatomical differences, love for a man or a woman is hardly another order of things — yet society has made of it something portentous, and we must expect homosexuals to accept this importance in stressing their identity. (Altman 1971, 219)

For these reasons, many homosexuals experience the homosexual identity as a transsituational identity at various times and places, an awareness of being carried from one situation to another.

The essentialist (Plummer 1981a, 1984), or sex-orientation (Plummer 1981b), approach to homosexuality is etiological, focusing primarily on sexual orientation and its development. Homosexuality is regarded as an orientation rather than a behavior. Essentialist concerns are reflected in research and writing on sexual preference by Bell, Weinberg, and Hammersmith (1981a, 1981b); Green (1974, 1976, 1979, 1987); Harry (1982, 1984/1985); Saghir and Robins (1973); Whitam (1977a, 1977b, 1980, 1981); Whitam and Mathy (1986); and Whitam and Zent (1984). Among sociologists, Whitam and Harry have emerged as the most vocal champions of the sex-orientation position.

The essentialist perspective differs from the social-construction and social-role frameworks in its use of the term *homosexual;* its view of what homosexuality represents; its use of the consistency principle; its explanations of departures from the consistency principle; and its preoccupation with childhood indicators of adult sexual preference.

Use of the Term Homosexual

From the essentialist perspective, the term *homosexual* is used as a noun. *Homosexual* describes an essence, a form of being, a specific type of sexual orientation:

> The formulation of homosexual orientation as biologically derived and therefore immutable, appearing in all societies at about the same rate, characterized by similar elements [e.g., cross-gendered behavior in childhood] in different societies, is more scientifically accurate than other contemporary formulations. (Whitam and Mathy 1986, 182)

From the vantage point of sexual-orientation, homosexuality and heterosexuality are two essentially different configurations. Different inner compositions, hormonally induced, generate different sexual orientations. Homosexuals and heterosexuals differ internally in the sense that apples differ from oranges and diamonds differ from rubies.

101

The constructionist and essentialist frameworks are superficially similar in that each uses the word *homosexual* as a noun. In contrast to the essentialists, however, identity-construct theorists argue

> that homosexuality is not a universal essence. Human gender and human sexuality is a diffuse open-ended matrix of potential possibility — to be narrowed down and organized in specific ways by specific sociohistorical formations. How we think, feel and act out our "sexualities" will depend on the ways that family structures set boundaries to emotional development, and the wider society sets boundaries to cognitive categories. (Plummer 1981a, 95)

Essentialists view sexual preference as an *actual* essence rather than as a *constructed* essence.

What Homosexuality Represents

From an extreme sex-orientation perspective, homosexuality has several key properties: It is present in all societies in approximately the same proportions; its meanings are eternal — that is, what homosexuality is, what it means to be homosexual, and the manner of homosexual expression are fixed and unchanging; sexual feelings rather than sexual behavior constitute the basis for sexual preference, which is established before birth; and homosexual identities are the inevitable product of homosexual preferences.

From an essentialist viewpoint, homosexuality is a universal essence that transcends time and place:

> Regardless of other manifestations of homosexuality, such as ritualistic homosexuality or secondary sexual activity, populations of homosexual persons emerge in all societies. (Whitam and Mathy 1986, 3)

Essentialists argue that homosexuality, an essential form of being, is experienced in much the same fashion wherever or whenever it occurs. Sexual arousal and activity with either sex is the same today as it was in ancient Greece:

> While it is difficult to know with certainty what psychological meanings the Greeks placed upon homosexuality, it is more reasonable to assume, unless there is clear evidence to the con-

trary, that the meaning of sexual activity between two homosexuals in ancient Greece does not differ significantly from the
meaning of similar relations in modern Greece or in other coun-
tries of the world. (Whitam and Mathy 1986, 17)

For essentialists, sexual feelings are a more accurate barometer of sexual orientation (i.e., essence) than sexual behavior. Harry (1984/1985)
argues, for example, that misclassification and conceptual imprecision
would be reduced if people with homosexual experiences (behaviors) were
differentiated from people with homosexual preferences (feelings):

> Many men within Kinsey's allegedly homosexual sample were
> essentially heterosexuals who, due to imprisonment, availed
> themselves of opportunities for homosexual contact. Also
> misclassified would be Reiss's (1961) adolescents who occa-
> sionally earned money through letting adult male homosexuals
> fellate them as long as the latter asked for no sexual reciproca-
> tion and expressed no affection. Further misclassified would be
> those married homosexual men who fantasize about males while
> having sex with their wives, and must do so to perform sexually.
> (p. 112)

Harry (1984/1985) uses nonerotic motives to explain instances where individuals' sexual feelings are at odds with their sexual behaviors: "There are
a variety of reasons for having sex other than erotic attraction. These can
include money, curiosity, pressure to conform, and availability" (p. 113).

From an essentialist perspective, homosexuals or heterosexuals are
"best defined in terms of attitudes or preferences rather than sexual
behavior" (Harry 1984/1985, 111). Accordingly, homosexuals are women
and men with homosexual feelings or preferences, rather than people who
engage in homosexual behavior. They are individuals who "exclusively or
nearly exclusively *prefer* partners of the same-sex for most of their adult
lives" (Whitam and Mathy 1986, 2; italics added). Homosexuals are people
who occupy position 6 or 5 on the Kinsey scale described in Chapter 2.

The bases for adult sexual preferences and for childhood (and sometimes adult) gender behavior are thought to reside in biological events experienced before birth:

> Nonetheless, our findings are not inconsistent with what one
> would expect to find if, indeed, there were a biological basis for
> sexual preference. If there is a biological basis for homosexuality,
> it probably accounts for gender nonconformity as well as sexual
> orientation. (Bell, Weinberg, and Hammersmith 1981a, 216-17)

Although sex-orientation research and scholarship have focused primarily on the development of sexual preference, they also contain an implicit image of homosexual identity. To essentialists, sexual feelings and preferences are more than labels; they exist independently of labels applied by the self or by others. "The label applied by individuals to their sexual orientation may not be consistent with the orientation" (Harry 1984/1985, 111-12). For essentialists, "learning sexuality entails learning what one really is. People can be unaware of this 'real' being—in which case they remain cases of 'latency' " (Plummer 1981a, 95). People express their "true" sexual natures when their sexual feelings match the labels they apply to those feelings. Labeling mirrors rather than constructs their sexual realities. Homosexual identities are formed when people acknowledge their "true" sexual feelings, whether or not they act on them.

The Consistency Principle

I use the term *sexual schema* to refer to the sexual component of self. Sexual schemas have *external* and *internal* dimensions. The external dimensions express the internal elements.

The external dimensions of sexual schemas are *biological sex, gender, gender role,* and *sexual behavior.* Although the terms sex and gender commonly are used interchangeably, Money (1985) defines *sex* as a person's *biological* status as a male or a female and *gender* as a person's *legal* status as a male or a female. *Gender role* refers to sets of external activities that express to self and others the degree to which one is male or female as culturally defined (i.e., masculine, feminine, or androgynous). The concept of gender role has been labeled alternatively as *social sex role* (Shively and De Cecco 1978). *Sexual behavior* refers to activities intended to produce sexual arousal or orgasm.

The internal dimensions of sexual schemas are *anatomic identity* (Green 1987), *gender identity, sexual orientation* (Money 1985), *sexual fantasy,* and *sexual identity.* *Anatomic identity* is a perception of self as male or female. *Gender identity* is the inner, private experience of gender role, a perception of self as masculine, feminine, or androgynous. *Sexual orientation* is an eroticized preference for a particular sex, and *sexual fantasy* refers to the mental images that elicit or sustain sexual arousal (Masters, Johnson, and Kolodny 1985). *Sexual identity* is an individual's perception of self as heterosexual, homosexual, or bisexual in relation to sexual or romantic settings.

Much of essentialist writing and research focuses on explaining departures from the *consistency principle,* which assumes that heterosexuality is the biological norm and that the internal and external components of sexual schemas cohere naturally and consistently. Given any single element, all other elements are "presumed to follow or co-occur" in a consonant fashion (Ponse 1978, 26). Thus, according to the consistency principle, legal males (gender and biological sex) see and experience themselves as male and masculine (anatomic and gender identity), behave in male-associated ways (gender role), prefer the opposite sex erotically (sexual orientation), have sexual fantasies that involve the opposite sex (sexual fantasy), view themselves as heterosexual (sexual identity), and express these components through heterosexual activity (sexual behavior). In a similar vein, legal females look upon themselves as female and feminine, act in feminine ways, find males sexually exciting, have opposite-sex sexual fantasies, conceive of themselves as heterosexual, and express these elements through sexual relations with males.

Departures from the Consistency Principle

All current formulations of the essentialist model share the basic assumption that people develop their sexual orientations early in life. Bell, Weinberg, and Hammersmith (1981a), and Whitam and Mathy (1986), for example, treat sexual preference as present at birth. Harry (1982) argues that sexual orientations grow out of gender-role preferences established during a period of childhood amnesia, between age two and age six. Essentialist writers currently regard sexual orientation as a fixed and enduring aspect of personality and treat homosexual preferences as naturally occurring departures from the consistency principle. Recent essentialist writers and investigators have sought to explain the development of homosexual preferences in terms of psychodynamic conditions, hormonal irregularities, and prenatal hormones.

Psychodynamic Conditions

Until the 1970s, the dominant psychodynamic approach toward homosexuality was psychoanalytic. This perspective classifies most lesbians and gay males as *obligatory,* or "true," homosexuals. True homosexuality is caused by psychic pain and developmental conflicts, and is likened to a disease:

> True obligatory homosexuality is a form of psychiatric or emotional illness. There is no obligatory homosexual who can be considered to be healthy. The very existence of this condition precludes it. (Socarides 1970, 1200-01)

For the most part, traditional psychoanalysis ignored lesbianism, and concentrated on explaining obligatory homosexuality in males.

In his reformulated theory of homosexuality, Socarides (1978) describes three forms: obligatory or preoedipal (consisting of types 1 and 2), oedipal, and schizo-homosexuality. He argues that obligatory homosexuality differs essentially from situational, variational, and latent forms. In addition, he asserts that most adult homosexuality is preoedipal because it is "unconsciously motivated and arises from anxiety," and is characterized by a "primary feminine identification," a "fear of engulfment [by the mother], ego dissolution, and loss of self and ego boundaries," and by "castration fears" (Socarides 1978, 91- 101). Bieber et al. (1962) made essentially the same point when they stated:

> We consider homosexuality to be a pathologic, biosocial, psychosexual adaptation to pervasive fears surrounding the expression of heterosexual impulses. All psychoanalytic theories assume that adult homosexuality is psychopathologic. (p. 18, 220)

From a psychoanalytic perspective, homosexuality is pathological because it results from a *derailing of heterosexual destiny*. Because a homosexual does not perform heterosexually, his or her heterosexual functioning is thought to be "crippled," like the legs of a polio victim. Analysts believe that it is not "normal" for a man to make love with another man, or a woman with another woman. Same-sex preferences occur only as a result of severely traumatizing childhood experiences. The flight from the opposite sex to the same sex is viewed as a *substitutive adaptation* (Goode 1984).

From a psychoanalytical perspective, homosexuality is a kind of failed heterosexuality, or a heterosexual inadequacy. It is a consequence of pathological fears of the opposite sex. "I suggest that homosexuality be characterized as a type of sexual inadequacy since most homosexuals cannot function heterosexually" (Bieber et al. 1962, 10, 12). In a similar vein, Socarides (1972) notes:

> The obligatory homosexual is unable to function in the most meaningful relationship in life: the male-female sexual union and the affective state of love, tenderness and joy with a partner of the opposite sex. The male's inability to function heterosexually and his extreme hostility toward women, originating in the fear of hostile and incestuous impulses toward the mother, have produced a wholesale flight from all females. (p. 121-22)

The causes of lesbianism have been similarly pathologized. According to Freud, lesbianism is caused by too strong an attachment to the father; incest fears involving the father are transferred to all men. Other psychoanalytic theories have located the causes of lesbianism in "oral eroticism," "fear of mutilation by pregnancy and childbirth," "fear of the opposite sex," or "clitoral fixation," to name only a few (Ponse 1978). Like the theories offered to explain male homosexuality, they remain unsupported by empirical evidence.

The pathological view of homosexuality fell into disrepute because of increasing acceptance of Kinsey's homosexual-heterosexual continuum, as well as his arguments that homosexuals and heterosexuals differ in degree (choice of object) rather than in kind (different psychological conditions) and that homosexuality is a naturally occurring variation.

Although psychoanalysts such as Bieber and Socarides denied the validity of Kinsey's continuum, most of their colleagues were not convinced by their objections. Evelyn Hooker's (1957, 1958) pioneering study of matched homosexual and heterosexual samples represented an early and significant break with the view that homosexuality and heterosexuality are separate psychological conditions and that heterosexuals and homosexuals have strikingly different levels of psychological adjustment. Hooker asked a panel of psychiatrists and clinical psychologists to differentiate homosexual and heterosexual subjects on the basis of their test scores on several measures of personality adjustment. The panel could do no better than to guess, indicating either that standardized tests are unable to measure homosexual/heterosexual personality differences or that no such differences exist. Based on these results, Hooker concluded that homosexuality falls within the normal range of psychological functioning. Later studies replicated Hooker's results (Freedman 1971; Green 1972; Hopkins 1969; Saghir and Robins 1973; Siegelman 1972, 1979; Thompson et al. 1971).

The demise of the pathology model may be shown most clearly by the omission of homosexuality from the third edition of the American Psychiatric Association's *Diagnostic and Statistical Manual of Mental Disorders* (DMS-III), published in 1980. After 1974, the APA no longer regarded homosexuality as a form of mental illness in itself. Today, psychiatrists are concerned only with people whose homosexuality is *ego-dystonic*—that is, individuals who experience difficulty in accepting their homosexual impulses. The position formerly held by psychoanalysts—that homosexuality is an essential difference caused by some kind of disorder—is now occupied by researchers who locate the causes of homosexuality in hormonal irregularities or prenatal hormonal disturbances.

Hormonal Irregularities

Recent research from a medical perspective has posited the origins of homosexuality in hormonal irregularities. As Tourney (1980) notes, some recent studies have found abnormal ratios of two breakdown products of testosterone — etiocholanolone and androsterone — in urine samples collected from both male and female homosexuals. These abnormal ratios have been offered as a possible explanation for homosexuality. Because females typically exhibit reduced A/E ratios (less androsterone than etiocholanolone), relatively high levels of androsterone are considered a possible cause of sexual preference for females in either sex. Similarly, because males typically exhibit increased A/E ratios (more androsterone than etiocholanolone), relatively low androsterone values are regarded as a possible cause of sexual preference for males in either sex.

Other studies have found that homosexuality is associated with the levels of male and female hormones in an individual's blood plasma. Tourney cites research that found lower plasma testosterone levels and sperm counts in exclusively or predominantly homosexual males and higher testosterone concentrations in the blood plasma of homosexual females than in heterosexual controls. Attempts to replicate hormonal studies, however, confused rather than clarified the original results. As Tourney notes, some investigators found no significant differences between homosexual and heterosexual subjects in testosterone levels or A/E ratios; others found significantly higher testosterone levels in exclusively homosexual male subjects. In addition, all these studies were based on the questionable assumption that homosexuality and heterosexuality are homogeneous, uniform categories (Birke 1981).

Present research into the role of hormones in homosexuality is more suggestive than definitive. Although some exclusively homosexual males exhibit low testosterone levels and some lesbians show elevated testosterone values, the majority do not. These hormonal differences, however, may be related not to homosexuality but to age, use of medication, use of alcohol or marijuana, sexually transmitted disease, diet, physical illness (Tourney 1980), stress, sexual stimulation, or diurnal rhythms (Birke 1981). It remains to be seen what these hormonal differences mean in those who exhibit them, and whether they cause or result from homosexual behavior.

Tourney sees the need for comprehensive studies in hormones and homosexuality to clarify what has become a confused collection of research reports. He suggests that future hormonal research use only exclusive homosexuals (Kinsey's 6s) who are free from disease; match experimental subjects and controls for height, age, weight, intelligence, education, and drug use; use larger samples and samples drawn from nonmedical and nonpsychiatric populations; take in-depth sexual histories; analyze androgens (male hormones), estrogens (female hormones), and gonadotrophins (hormones that stimulate hormone production) in blood plasma rather than in urine; and take into account the menstrual cycle and other related hormonal changes when examining female homosexuals.

In summarizing research on a possible link between homosexuality and hormonal functioning, Meyer-Bahlburg (1977, 1979) concluded that evidence supporting a hormonal basis for male homosexuality is weak. Further, the majority of female homosexuals appear to have testosterone and estrogen levels that fall within the normal range, although a significant minority, roughly one-third, exhibit elevated testosterone levels.

Prenatal Hormones

The hypothalamus is a structure in the brain that governs the production of sex hormones. Some researchers believe that the circumstances surrounding its development determine gender behavior and adult sexual preferences. The hypothalamus develops in two phases. The first phase, thought to occur between the fourth and seventh month of fetal development, is a critical period of differentiation; at that time the hypothalamus becomes physiologically organized and sensitized. Androgen (male hormone) levels are crucial to this differentiation; the relative presence or absence of androgens both shapes the hypothalamus and determines how it responds to hormones. The second phase occurs at puberty, when the hypothalamus is activated either by androgens or by estrogens. Dörner (1976, 1977) theorizes that during the first phase, the male hormone organizes the hypothalamic center in a fashion that produces masculine behavior postnatally. Conversely, the absence of androgens is thought to differentiate the hypothalamus physiologically in a fashion that produces feminine behavior postnatally.

Dörner's research on hamsters and rats generated the hypothesis of a neuroendocrine basis for homosexuality and bisexuality in humans. Male rats with a temporary androgen deficiency during hypothalamic development, but with normal androgen levels at maturity, were aroused sexually by other male rats. Neuroendocrine-induced male homosexuality was prevented if androgens were administered during the first phase of hypothalamic organization. Female rats with a temporary androgen excess during hypothalamic development were unable to ovulate and/or were predisposed to hyposexuality, bisexuality, or homosexuality at maturity. The higher the androgen level during hypothalamic sensitization, the more stereotypically male the behavior at maturity, regardless of genetic sex. Conversely, the lower the androgen level during hypothalamic differentiation, the more stereotypically female the behavior at maturity, regardless of genetic sex.

Dörner obtained evidence supporting the hypothesis that androgen-deficient male rats possess "female differentiated" brains by observing their responses to estrogen injections; the rats exhibited a "positive estrogen feedback" effect similar to those exhibited by "normal" female rats. An initial decrease in serum-luteinizing hormone (LH) levels was followed by an increase above initial LH values. When nonandrogen-deficient adult male rats were injected with estrogens, they exhibited initial decreases in serum LH levels that were not followed by an increase over original LH levels.

Dörner et al. (1975) conducted an experiment on male homosexuals to determine whether they had "female-differentiated brains," that is, whether they exhibited a positive estrogen feedback after being injected with estrogens. All twenty-one of the exclusively homosexual males who participated in the experiment exhibited positive estrogen feedback within twenty-four hours of receiving estrogen injections. By contrast, the twenty heterosexual and five bisexual men in the control group exhibited decreases in serum LH levels within the twenty-four hours after injections without subsequent increases above initial LH values. Analyses of the subjects' plasma and urinary testosterone levels showed no differences between heterosexual and homosexual subjects. On the basis of this study, Dörner and his associates (1975) concluded that male homosexuality and bisexuality are probably caused by prenatal androgen deficiencies (female-differentiated hypothalamus):

> The elicitation of a positive estrogen feedback effect in the majority of intact homosexual men in contrast to intact heterosexual men suggests that homosexual men may possess, at least in part, a predominantly female-differentiated brain. This may be caused by an absolute or relative androgen deficiency during the critical hypothalamic organizational phase in prenatal life. A normal or at least approximately normal androgen level during the post pubertal hypothalamic phase may then activate the predominantly female-differentiated brain of a genetic and somatophenotypic male to homosexual behavior. (p. 6)

By analogy, female homosexuality and bisexuality result from androgen overdoses—and thus from male-differentiated brains—during the critical prenatal phase of hypothalamic sensitization.

The Dörner et al. (1975) research is seriously flawed. First, the results were partially confounded because of the way in which the experimental samples were stratified. Some of the homosexual males, for example, were placed in the homosexual rather than the bisexual category, even though they had heterosexual experience; the sexual histories of the controls were not described; and the homosexual subjects were not representative of homosexuals as a group. (At the time of the study, for example, all the homosexual subjects were hospitalized for the treatment of skin disorders or sexually transmitted disease, which may alter hormonal functioning.)

Replication would have been facilitated, and more rigorous and accurate comparison between homosexual, heterosexual, and bisexual subjects would have been possible, if the Kinsey scale had been used as a basis for classifying people as homosexual (6 and 5), bisexual (2 to 4), or heterosexual (0 and 1). There is at present no way of determining how well the subjects represented the sexual-orientation categories to which they were assigned (Carrier 1975).

In addition, Dörner et al. do not describe the gender characteristics of their experimental samples. Did the subjects assigned to each sex-orientation category run the gamut from masculine to feminine in their gender behaviors, or were only effeminate males represented in the homosexual category and masculine males in the heterosexual category? Moreover, the investigators do not define what they mean by the terms "female-like" and "male-like" behavior. Because they describe homosexual behavior as "predominantly female-like," I suspect that only effeminate male homosexuals were represented in the homosexual category. It would be interesting to know whether effeminate and masculine exclusively homosexual males would exhibit equally strong positive-estrogen feedback (Carrier 1975).

Van Wyk (1984) and Hoult (1983/1984) have leveled the most incisive criticisms against the Dörner et al. (1975) study. According to the Dörner group, the LH levels of all male subjects dropped below baseline levels within twenty-four hours of receiving estrogen injections. Within seventy-two to ninety-six hours after injection, however, the LH levels of homosexuals rose above baseline, while those of the bisexual and heterosexual men did not, demonstrating a positive estrogen feedback effect in homosexual males. Thus, to be consistent with the theoretical view that prenatal androgen deficits foster homosexual preferences in males, bisexual males injected with estrogens should have exhibited LH levels between those exhibited by male homosexual and heterosexual subjects.

Van Wyk reanalyzed the Dörner et al. data and concluded that the theory was seriously flawed. First, testosterone levels for bisexual subjects were not presented, making it difficult to interpret the data on that group. Second, ninety-six hours after injection, when the LH levels of homosexuals had reached their above-baseline peak and when those of the heterosexuals had returned to baseline, the LH levels for bisexuals remained significantly below baseline. This result seriously compromised the theory proposing a link between hypothalamic development and adult homosexuality:

> These bisexual males appear to have hypermasculinized brains,
> which, however, do not impel them to seek exclusively female
> sex partners. Given this additional behavioral fact (that they are

bisexual), their [Dörner et al.] interpretation is not well supported by the data they offer. (Van Wyk 1984, 413)

Hoult (1983/1984) details additional problems with the Dörner et al. study: (1) The small sample size prohibits meaningful generalizations; and (2) close scrutiny of the data reveals that positive estrogen feedback-effects actually occurred in only one-third of the male homosexual subjects:

Seventy-seven percent of the [positive estrogen feedback effect] was due to the extreme reactions of 7 of 20 men. On the other hand, 10 of the 20 heterosexual men accounted for all of what may be termed the "negative feedback effect" found in the heterosexual group. The average negative result achieved with the bisexual men was far larger than the average achieved with the heterosexual men. (Hoult 1983/1984, 145)

In conclusion, prenatal hormone deficiencies or excesses have been linked to adult homosexuality in only a few instances. Human females with adrenogenital syndrome, for example, a condition caused by prenatal androgen excesses, may be predisposed to develop homosexual preferences as adults (Ehrhardt, Evers, and Money 1968). Similar reports have been made regarding homosexual preferences in males with Klinefelter's syndrome, a condition caused by a prenatal androgen deficiency (Masters, Johnson, and Kolodny 1985). These cases are atypical, however; they have little relevance to sexual development in general or to the sexual development of homosexual adults, who rarely display these physical anomalies. Meyer-Bahlburg (1984) succinctly summarizes current thought on the role of hormones in the development of sexual preference and gender behavior:

Gender development or psychosexual differentiation—i.e., the formation of sex-dimorphic behavior, gender identity, and sexual orientation—is a complex process spanning many years. It probably involves several sensitive developmental periods, specific to certain behavioral categories, and is open to modifying influences throughout life. (p. 391)

Predicting Adult Sexual Preferences

Several recent studies have attempted to determine whether certain constellations of childhood behaviors predict adult homosexual preferences (Bell, Weinberg, and Hammersmith 1981a; Green 1974, 1976, 1979, 1987; Harry 1982; Saghir and Robins 1973; Whitam 1977a, 1977b, 1980, 1981;

Whitam and Mathy 1986; Whitam and Zent 1984). These studies examined the relationship between childhood gender-role preferences and adult sexual orientations. In general, the results revealed significant differences between homosexuals and heterosexuals in their childhood gender-role interests and behaviors. Although the gender identities and roles of most homosexual adults are consistent with their biological sex, they are more likely than heterosexual controls to recall having had sex-inappropriate interests and behaviors during childhood (Harry 1982).

Saghir and Robins's (1973) study of noninstitutionalized American male and female homosexuals was one of the first to report a link between gender-inappropriate childhood behaviors and adult homosexuality. More than two-thirds (67%) of their male homosexual subjects ($N = 72$), as compared to 3 percent ($N = 1$) of their male heterosexual controls ($N = 35$), described themselves as having been "girl-like" during childhood. This "girl-like" description included a preference for girls' toys and games, a preference for female playmates, and an avoidance of rough-and-tumble, aggressive boyhood play. Twenty-seven percent ($N = 18$) of the male homosexuals but only 3 percent ($N = 1$) of the male heterosexual controls wanted to be girls (change their sex) as children; 37 percent of the male homosexuals ($N = 33$), compared to 23 percent ($N = 8$) of the heterosexual males, had ever cross-sex dressed. "Among boys destined to become adult male homosexuals, the prevalence of polysymptomatic effeminacy is very high" (Saghir and Robins 1973, 18).

The fifty-six homosexual females interviewed by Saghir and Robins exhibited a similar cross-gendered pattern as children. Whereas more than two-thirds (70%) of the female homosexuals recalled tomboyish childhood behavior, only 16 percent of the forty-three heterosexual controls had similar recollections. In addition, more than half of the homosexual females, but none of the heterosexual tomboys, persisted with "tomboyism" into adolescence. The "boy-like" syndrome included a preference for boys' toys, male playmates, "masculine-type" activities, and an absence of interest in "girl-oriented" and domestic activities such as sewing, cooking, and doll play. A majority of the homosexual women (63%) but only a minority of the controls (7%) reported having wanted to change their gender (to be boys) as children. Saghir and Robins conclude that tomboyishness is not altogether innocuous; a certain proportion of persistently tomboyish girls would probably develop homosexual orientations in adulthood.

Frederick Whitam's (1977a) questionnaire research on a sample of American male homosexuals ($N = 206$) and heterosexual controls ($N = 78$) found additional support for the hypothesis that "prehomosexual" children exhibit cross-gender preferences and behaviors. As children, the exclusive homosexuals in his sample ($N = 107$) were more likely than exclusive heterosexual controls ($N = 68$) to have been interested in dolls (47% vs.

0%), to have dressed in women's clothing (44% vs. 0%), to have preferred girls as playmates (42% vs. 2%) and older women as companions (61% vs. 13%), to have been labeled a "sissy" (29% vs. 2%), and to have preferred sex play with boys to sex play with girls (78% vs. 12%). Subsequent studies in Guatemala, Brazil, and the Philippines (Whitam 1980; Whitam and Zent 1984) replicated the original results. In summarizing these earlier results, Whitam and Mathy (1986) concluded "not only that homosexual orientation has a biological basis but that some aspects of gender behavior may also be biologically derived" (p. 157).

Bell, Weinberg, and Hammersmith's (1981a, 77-86, 147-59) research on the development of sexual preference also disclosed significant homosexual/heterosexual differences in the childhood gender-role preferences and behavior of American homosexuals. Homosexual males (N = 575), for example, were significantly less likely than heterosexual controls (N = 284) to describe themselves as "very masculine" (18% vs. 67%) as children, and significantly more likely to describe themselves as passive (22% vs. 8%) and submissive (20% vs. 3%).

Lesbians were also more likely than heterosexual controls to remember exhibiting cross-gender traits during childhood. Lesbians (N = 229), for example, were more likely (62% vs. 10%) than heterosexual controls (N = 101) to describe themselves as "very masculine" while they were growing up. In addition, the lesbians were more likely than heterosexual controls (33% vs. 21%) to describe themselves as "very dominant."

In addition to gender-inappropriate behaviors, male homosexuals were more likely than heterosexual controls to report gender-inappropriate interests. Only 11 percent of the homosexual males stated that they were "very much" interested in "boys' activities" (e.g., baseball, football) during grade school, as compared with 70 percent of the male heterosexual controls. Further, 37 percent of the homosexual males had cross-sex dressed (aside from school plays or Halloween) and pretended to be girls during grade school, compared to only 10 percent of the heterosexual controls. The homosexual males were also more likely than heterosexual controls (46% vs. 11%) to report having enjoyed "girlish" activities during childhood (e.g., hopscotch, playing house or jacks) "somewhat" or "very much."

Gender-inappropriate behaviors and interests also characterized the childhoods of the lesbian sample in the Bell, Weinberg, and Hammersmith (1981a) study. Lesbians (N = 229) were less likely (13% vs. 55%) than heterosexual controls (N = 101) to say they "very much" enjoyed typical girls' activities (e.g., hopscotch, playing house or jacks) during childhood. They were also more likely than heterosexual controls (71% vs. 28%) to say they "very much" enjoyed typical boys' activities, and were more likely than heterosexual controls (49% vs. 7%) to recall having dressed as boys and having pretended to be boys when they were growing up. Bell, Weinberg, and Hammersmith (1981a) conclude by saying:

> Among both men and the women in our study, there is a powerful link between gender nonconformity and the development of homosexuality. What we seem to have identified is a pattern of feelings and reactions within the child that cannot be traced back to a single social or psychological root; indeed, homosexuality may arise from a biological precursor (as do left-handedness and allergies, for example) that parents cannot control. (p. 188, 191-92)

Richard Green (1987) examined the link between childhood gender nonconformity and adult homosexuality in a fifteen-year longitudinal study. His subjects consisted of sixty-six "feminine" prepubescent boys and a matched control group of fifty-six "conventionally 'masculine' boys." According to parental reports, "sissies" were more likely than "conventional" boys to want to be a girl; to dress in female clothing; to play with dolls; to adopt a female role when playing house; to relate better to females than to males; to be a voluntary loner or to be rejected from male peer groups; and to be uninterested in "rough and tumble" play and sports.

Subjects were interviewed during childhood and again ten to fifteen years later during adolescence or young adulthood. One-third (33%) of the "feminine" boys and slightly more than one-third of the "conventional" boys (38%) dropped out over the course of the study. Subjects available for the follow-up interview were asked to describe

> the fantasies that excite during masturbation, the erotic images of nocturnal emissions, or "wet dreams," the types of pictorial pornography that induce erections, the percent of the time that erotic content involved male or female partners during the past year, experiences leading to orgasms with a single partner, or a sequence of solitary experiences with transient partners. (Green 1987, p. 99-100)

Each individual was assigned a Kinsey composite score based upon his reported sexual fantasies and activities. On the basis of this scale, twelve of the "feminine" boys were rated as heterosexual (Kinsey 0 or 1), fourteen were rated as bisexual (Kinsey 2, 3, or 4), and eighteen were rated as homosexual (Kinsey 5 or 6). Only one of the "conventional" boys was rated bisexual (Kinsey 2); none were rated as homosexual. The results led Green (1987) to conclude that " 'feminine' boys are far more likely to mature into homosexual or bisexual men than are most boys" (p. 99).

Joseph Harry's (1982) research on male homosexuals provides further support for the argument that cross-gender role preferences in childhood sometimes predict adult homosexual preferences. Forty-two percent ($N = 1581$) of the male homosexuals in this study reported being called "sissies" during childhood, compared to 11 percent ($N = 204$) of the heterosexual controls. In addition, 22 percent of the homosexual men recalled wanting to be girls as children, whereas this was true of only 5 percent of the heterosexual controls. The gay men in this sample were also significantly more likely than heterosexual controls (47% vs. 12%) to have preferred girls to boys as childhood companions, and to have cross-sex dressed as children (36% vs. 5%).

Harry (1982) also analyzes critically the works of Whitam (1977a), Saghir and Robins, and Bell, Weinberg, and Hammersmith (1981a). In these studies, he notes, it was assumed that homosexual preferences induce individuals to adopt cross-gender role preferences. Harry (1982) argues instead that cross-gender role preferences generate homosexual orientations:

> Studies of effeminate boys have shown that their cross-gender role-preferences appear to be largely established between the ages of two and six. These years seem to precede the years of crystallization of an erotic preference which typically occurs around puberty or thereafter. (p. 13)

To test the hypothesis that early gender-role preferences shape adult sexual orientations, Harry recalculated the percentages of the Whitam (1977a), Saghir and Robins, and Bell, Weinberg, and Hammersmith (1981a) data using childhood gender-role preference as the causal or the independent variable and sexual preference as the effect or the dependent variable. His reanalysis revealed "huge differences" between homosexuals and heterosexuals in childhood gender-role preferences; homosexual males were significantly more likely than heterosexual controls to have been cross-gendered during childhood. He concluded that "while a childhood cross-gender role-preference is not determinative of sexual orientation, it makes it more likely than not that the person will be gay" (Harry 1982, 13).

Harry (1982) also took issue with Bell, Weinberg, and Hammersmith's (1981a) conclusion that homosexuality arises from biological precursors:

> Finding that none of these [parental and peer influence] theories were confirmed, they concluded that the origins of sexual orientation are probably biological. Of course, the form of their argument is one of default. It assumes that one has tested and eliminated all possible or feasible environmental hypotheses. (p. 243)

The Essentialist Position: A Critique

All the studies discussed here, which examined the early gender-role preferences of homosexuals, asserted that cross-gender preferences during childhood predict adult homosexuality in both sexes. On the basis of research conducted in Brazil, Guatemala, the Philippines, and the United States, Whitam and Mathy (1986) conclude that cross-gender preferences in childhood are associated universally with adult homosexuality. The proponents of cross-gender preferences disagree only on the issue of causal ordering: whether homosexual orientations induce cross-gender role preferences, or whether cross-gender role preferences engender homosexual orientations.

Studies that link gender-inappropriate behavior among children with adult homosexuality may be questioned on several grounds. First, as I indicated earlier, the existing evidence does not provide solid support for the argument that there is a biological predisposition to homosexuality. The studies cited to bolster this claim are seriously flawed. Moreover, none of the researchers who argue that gender nonconformity is associated with future homosexuality measured the biological variables that they claim predispose people to gender nonconformity as children and to homosexuality as adults. Yet, even if homosexual orientations are determined fully by biology, the *meanings* of sexual feelings are neither self-evident nor translated directly into consciousness. People construct their sexual orientations; they actively interpret, define, and make sense of their erotic yearnings through systems of sexual meanings articulated by the wider culture.

Even Alan Bell, one of the major proponents of the sex-orientation model, found a biological explanation for sexual preference inadequate. After the publication of his co-researched sexual-preference study, Bell (1982) offered a social-learning explanation for the development of sexual orientations. He noted that he and his colleagues had neglected to ask the homosexuals in their study to indicate the meanings they attached to their homosexual feelings during adolescence. (The gay males in their study reported first feeling attracted to the same sex at an average age of thirteen; the corresponding figure for lesbians was an average age of sixteen.) Bell (1982) notes:

Informants' feelings of attraction often assumed the form of: romantic attachments to another, a yearning for contact, hope for a reciprocal interest on the other person's part, an idealization of that person. (p. 2)

Bell conceptualizes love as a desire to merge psychologically with the loved one, a search for completion, a desire to incorporate into the self components of masculinity or femininity that the love object is seen as possessing in greater abundance than the self. "Thus, a necessary ingredient for romantic attachment is one's perception of the loved one as essentially different from oneself in terms of gender-related attributes" (1982, 2). For both heterosexuals and homosexuals, according to Bell, people perceived as essentially different from the self are prime candidates for early romantic and later erotic investments.

Bell theorizes that gender-conforming boys and girls generally are accepted by, involved with, and feel close to same-sex peers during childhood. By the time they reach adolescence, gender conformists see members of the same sex as "finished business"; they no longer appear as sources of mystery and fascination. The idealization of the same sex has been tempered by realism. Members of the opposite sex, however, "viewed at a distance and experienced as far different from themselves, are suddenly discovered, as if for the first time, by early adolescence" (Bell 1982, 2).

Bell argues that the opposite set of developmental experiences characterizes the childhood and adolescent experiences of gender nonconformists. Disinterest in, or rejection and isolation from, same-sex peers in childhood generates an almost exclusive involvement and identification with the opposite sex. By adolescence, the opposite sex is "finished business," while the same sex is viewed as different, mysterious, and desirable.

Second, although Bell, Weinberg, and Hammersmith (1981a), and Whitam and Mathy (1986), treat homosexuality as a "natural," biologically derived variation, like left-handedness, the research they cite to support the biological position is not only flawed but views homosexuality as the outcome of a pathological condition: excessively high or low androgen levels during prenatal development. At the same time, these researchers reject the "pathological" position when they argue that homosexuality is a naturally occurring variation. De Cecco (1987) argues that their position

> unwittingly promotes the very intolerance of homosexuality they hope to alleviate through their research. The prejudice against homosexuality does not stem fundamentally from the simple rejection of homosexual acts and emotional reactions. This prejudice springs from the belief that homosexuals are not quite the men or women they ought to be and, in fact, are the females and males they ought not to be. (p.111)

Third, because people of both sexes range along a continuum of sexual responsiveness and behavior from complete heterosexuality through complete homosexuality, it is not surprising that exclusively homosexual adults *may be* found in roughly the same proportions (5%) in all societies

(Whitam and Mathy 1986). I say "may be found" because there is no way of determining whether five percent of all adults in all societies, past and present, were or are exclusively homosexual. Admittedly, a small proportion of people always occupy the extremes on any continuum. Sex-orientation researchers, however, treat individuals at the ends of the spectrum of sexual responsiveness and behavior as if they showed a difference in quality, not in degree. Thus the essentialists have constructed "the homosexual" (and "the heterosexual") by treating a difference of degree as if it were a difference in kind.

Fourth, although significant minorities of male and female homosexuals in the Bell, Weinberg, and Hammersmith (1981a), Harry (1982), and Whitam (1977a) studies were cross-gendered as children, a majority were not. Sixty-three percent of the male homosexuals, and 51 percent of the lesbians in the Bell, Weinberg, and Hammersmith (1981a) study did not cross-sex dress or pretend to be the opposite sex during childhood; and 54 percent of the gay males and 29 percent of the lesbians did not enjoy opposite-sex activities as children.

A similar trend is revealed in Harry's (1982) data. Fifty-eight percent of his male homosexual respondents did not recall being called sissies as children; 63 percent did not cross-sex dress during childhood; 78 percent did not want to be girls as children; and 53 percent preferred boys to girls as childhood playmates. Similarly, 53 percent of Whitam's (1977a) exclusive male homosexual subjects did not play with dolls as children; 66 percent did not cross-sex dress during childhood; 58 percent did not prefer girls as playmates; and 71 percent were not called "sissies."

I have no quarrel with the position that childhood gender nonconformity is *sometimes* associated with adult homosexuality among children raised in the United States or in societies with similar gender arrangements (e.g., Guatemala, Brazil, and the Philippines). Even so, the arguments that gender nonconformity causes homosexual orientations, or that homosexual orientations induce gender-inappropriate behaviors, are tautological or circular. Gender nonconformity is used in these cases to explain a form of gender nonconformity, namely, homosexual orientations. Richard Green's (1987) study provides an example of this sort of reasoning: "Feminine" boys, he argues, become gay adults. Yet, 59 percent of his "feminine" boys turned out to be heterosexual ($N = 12$) or bisexual ($N = 14$) in adolescence or young adulthood.

A fifth criticism of essentialism concerns methods. In the studies that found gender-inappropriate behavior to be typical of people who grew up to be homosexual, the heterosexual control groups were small relative to the homosexual samples with which they were compared. The controls may also have been less variable and more homogeneous, creating an impression of homosexual/heterosexual childhood differences that in fact do not exist, or exist to a lesser degree than the researchers found. In addition, Americans experience pressure to eliminate or suppress gender nonconformist tendencies beginning in childhood, and the control respondents may have been motivated defensively to deny such childhood behaviors:

> Proving one's manhood/womanhood is in the popular imagination bound up with the rejection of any fag or dyke characteristics. If this seems more obvious in the case of men, it is because women have traditionally been defined as inferior, and whereas there is some grudging respect accorded women with masculine qualities, none is given to "womanly" men. Even among children "tomboys" are more acceptable than "sissies." (Altman 1971, 69-70)

Finally, in societies where there is rigid differentiation between sex roles, such as the United States, homosexuals are portrayed stereotypically as displaying gender-inappropriate interests and actions. Lesbians and gay males raised in such societies are predisposed as adults to read gender-inappropriate themes into their childhood behaviors and interests. Homosexuals who grow up in societies with more flexible gender schemas are less likely to recall having displayed gender-inappropriate interests and actions as children (Ross 1980).

Conclusions

The ritualized homosexuality of the Sambia, the New Guinea tribe discussed in Chapter 5, sheds light on some of the weaknesses associated with the essentialist position. Ritualized homosexuality supports the constructionist argument that the meanings attached to sexual practices reflect historical time and sociocultural arrangements. The ways in which homosexual behaviors and feelings are experienced and expressed vary across time and place, as do ideas about what it means to be homosexual. Essentialists also routinely ignore the variability of meanings attributed to homosexuality and the varied forms that homosexuality assumes:

> Is the experience of two men in a New York Leather Bar beating each other comparable to the fantasies of de Sade? Is the paternalistic tutorship of boy and adult in ancient Greece the same as the "child molester" locked up in our modern prisons? Is the wearing of female costume by males in a modern Beaumont Society meeting in a provincial English town comparable to that of the Berdache? The actual meaning of the experience is orga-

nized so differently in each case that it is dangerous to render them too similar. (Plummer 1984, 223)

Sambian sexuality also demonstrates that most people possess the capacity to be emotionally and behaviorally bisexual if their culture institutionalizes both homosexual and heterosexual patterns. When heterosexuality and homosexuality are presented as valid alternatives rather than mutually exclusive conditions, most people can enjoy both patterns, even though they may prefer one option to the other. Sambian sexuality also illustrates the risks of using sexual behavior as a basis for classifying people as homosexual or heterosexual; all Sambian males engage in homosexual behavior, but only a tiny minority are not committed exclusively to heterosexual patterns as adults.

Sambian sexual expression also suggests that in any given society a small minority will be homosexually oriented:

> The total number of these [Sambian] "deviants" probably constitutes no more than 5 percent of the entire male population. Some of these homosexually oriented men, after marriage and fatherhood, still continue to engage in homosexual activities even though they are disparaged for doing so. Please note, however, that they act only as inserters, not as fellators of younger boys — which is strictly forbidden, is immoral, and would be regarded as unspeakably unmanly. (I know of only two reported instances of older males acting as fellators for younger males, out of scores of cases investigated.) (Herdt 1981, 252ff)

Sambian culture views all young boys as cross-gendered, essentially feminine. For this reason, early separation from maternal (feminine) influences and ritualized homosexual practices are deemed essential to a boy's masculinization. Effeminacy is acceptable in small children, but the male ritual eliminates or reduces "girlish" behaviors in boys to ensure "normal masculine development." Through these practices, all boys gain experiences with the masculine role, as defined by Sambian culture; they are not characterized as either feminine or masculine, but as one first and then as the other.

The Western idea that masculinity and femininity are mutually exclusive, that one is either masculine or feminine but not both, limits people's chances to develop both kinds of roles. Cross-gender preferences are stigmatized; there are no socially sanctioned opportunities to experiment with masculine and feminine gender roles in supportive contexts; young gender nonconformists are rejected socially. As my discussion has shown, the essentialists' preoccupation with possible links between cross-gender role preferences in childhood and adult homosexuality reveals more about the construction and interpretation of gender in the West than about the development of homosexual orientations.

Chapter **8**   CONCLUSION

Two themes have prevailed in this book: first, that sexual conduct is primarily social, and second, that professional thinking about sexuality in general, and homosexuality and homosexual identity in particular, is undergoing constant change. In the United States, societywide shifts in conceptions of sex and gender have been associated with changes in professional perceptions of homosexuals.

Sexual Conduct as Social in Origin

As indicated in Chapter 2, sexual conduct is primarily social in origin. Existing sociocultural arrangements define what sexuality is, the purposes it serves, its manner of expression, and what it means to be sexual. This statement does not deny a biological substratum to human sexuality, but emphasizes the powerful role of social forces in shaping sexual conduct. When I say that sexual conduct is "constructed," I mean that it is organized and expressed through sexual scripts or erotic codes — that is, through social roles.

Sexual scripts are like blueprints; they channel and focus sexual conduct, thereby providing sexuality with its cognitive and affective boundaries. Sexual scripts set the cognitive limits of sexuality by defining the who, what, when, where, why, and how of sexual expression. Because the meanings of sexual feelings are neither self-evident nor translated directly into consciousness, these scripts or codes fix the emotional boundaries of sexuality by specifying what kinds of feelings are sexual. People construct their sexual feelings to the extent that they use systems of sexual meanings articulated by the wider culture to interpret, define, and make sense of their erotic yearnings. The constructed nature of sexual identity was illustrated by the model of homosexual identity formation presented in Chapter 4.

Sexual scripts exist at three distinct levels: the cultural, the interpersonal, and the intrapsychic. The impact of cultural scenarios on sexual expression has been emphasized throughout this book. In contemporary America, the cultural scenario contains three different sexual scripts: the procreative, the relational, and the recreational. Because sexual learning occurs within specific historical eras and sociocultural settings, sexual con-

123

duct and its meanings vary through history and among cultures. The social-role and social-construction perspectives, discussed in Chapters 5 and 6, emphasize the cultural and historical relativity of conceptions of homosexuality.

"The Homosexual" as Social Construct

Because homosexuals are defined by (and define) dominant groups and institutions within the wider culture, their images are constituted socially and are subject to cultural and historical change. Lesbian and gay male sexuality is also constructed socially; it is organized and expressed through homosexual scripts. In Chapter 5, the social-role perspective showed that in the West, institutions in the homosexual community articulate and inform homosexual scripts. Both social-construction and social-role theorists argue that even if homosexual feelings themselves are not learned, the erotic codes or roles that express them are the product of social learning.

Over the past several hundred years, Western conceptualizations of homosexuality have undergone major transformations. Paradigmatic shifts have altered images of what homosexuality is, what it means to be homosexual, what homosexuals are like, and what the causes of homosexuality are. The historical record in Chapter 5 shows the changes in the frameworks used to explain the empirical reality of homosexuality. As one theoretical approach failed, rival frameworks emerged which claimed to explain the phenomenon more fully. At various times, homosexuality in America has been defined as a sin, as a disease, as an alternative lifestyle and minority status, and, most recently, as a health threat.

Homosexuality as Sin

In the Judeo-Christian West, homosexuality was regarded traditionally as a behavior. Because the Bible prohibits "every form of sexual activity other than heterosexual, genital intercourse" (Szasz 1970, 160), non-procreative sexual options such as homosexuality, masturbation, and oral genital contact were constructed as sinful, and the practitioners were labeled heretics.

In the late nineteenth century, secular rather than sacred interpretations of sexuality began to gain social currency. Social and medical conceptualizations of sexuality replaced religious and moral perspectives. Medicine wrested control of sexuality from religion, and doctors replaced priests "as the new guardians of social conduct and morality" (Szasz 1970, 160). The emerging discipline of psychiatry colonized the province of sexual health and disease; it cloaked moral and sexual issues in the rhetoric of science. In the name of scientific progress, sin was redefined as sickness, heresy as mental illness, and moral sanction as medical treatment (Szasz 1970).

Homosexuality as Disease

Although psychiatric dogma supplanted religious doctrine as the ultimate arbiter of sexual decorum, Judeo-Christian teachings and philosophy remained an ingrained part of psychotherapeutic thought. Like religious doctrine, psychiatric dogma was hostile toward nonprocreative sexuality; it endorsed standards of gender and sexual expression anchored in procreative concerns. From a procreative perspective, women and men are intrinsically different: A woman's primary role is motherhood (childbearing and childrearing) and a man's primary role is that of bread-winner. According to traditional psychiatry, procreation is the only legitimate sexual use for the body, and nonprocreative options are deviant. Men marry to obtain regular sex; women barter sex for marriage. Open and unregulated sexuality threatens this arrangement (Luker 1984). The American Psychiatric Association's *Diagnostic and Statistical Manual: I,* first published in the 1950s, defined masturbation, fellatio, cunnilingus, homosexuality, and "uncontrolled sexuality"—Don Juanism and nymphomania—as forms of mental illness (Levine and Troiden 1986).

Because medical thought transformed religious principles into pseudo-scientific diagnostic terms, the language of disease or abnormality replaced the language of sin in evaluations of nonprocreative options; moral judgment was camouflaged by medical diagnosis (Szasz 1980). The focus of homosexuality research became etiological; because homosexuality was viewed as a disease, researchers sought to determine its causes. Genetic, hormonal, developmental, and familial factors were examined—and abandoned—as explanations.

Homosexuality as Minority Status

Nontraditional perspectives toward sex and gender emerged in the 1960s and early 1970s. The sexual revolution and the rise of the counter-culture cast doubt on traditional images of women and men, and challenged the institutional dominance of the procreative ethic. Reinforced by the self-fulfillment ethic and current feminist ideologies, contemporary standards of sex and gender defined women and men as substantially similar (equal) rather than different, women as sexual rather than asexual, and mother-hood as an option rather than as a primary role (Luker 1984).

Americans, mostly those who were urban, young, educated, and middle-class, were exposed to relational, recreational, and procreative standards of sexuality. Both relational and recreational scripts portray sexuality as something to be enjoyed, although the two scripts differ in the level of commitment required for sexual intimacy. Relational scripts approve of erotic contact in committed, love-based unions. Recreational scripts do not demand commitment as a prerequisite for sexual intimacy; they define sex as play, with mutual pleasure as the goal and no commitment beyond the moment.

A generation of Americans was exposed to erotic codes that endorsed sexual liberation and free love, and supported the abandonment of a procreative ethic (Yankelovich 1974, 1981). People's ties to an ethic of sexual restraint were weakened further by advances in contraceptive technology (e.g., oral contraceptives); legalized abortion; and the availability of new, potent antibiotics for the treatment of sexually transmitted diseases. The general atmosphere of societal permissiveness was supercharged in the gay urban ghettos throughout the nation; the gay male community evolved into a sexual hothouse (Levine and Troiden 1986). For some, the sexual marketplace expanded from informal parties and gay bars to gay baths, backroom bars, parks, and tearooms. Sexual promiscuity became a way of life, as well as a form of recreation (Altman 1982).

Gay liberation introduced a political dimension to professional and lay discourse on homosexuality. Armed with research results, lesbian and gay political activists and progressive mental-health professionals clamored for changes in the legal, medical, and psychiatric definitions of homosexuality. Because research had demonstrated that homosexuals fall within the normal range psychologically, the American Psychiatric Association removed ego-syntonic homosexuality from its list of mental disorders in 1974. Several states passed legislation decriminalizing homosexual relations between consenting adults.

The mental-health establishment, if not the wider society, had redefined homosexuality as an alternative lifestyle and homosexuals as members of a minority (Altman 1982). When professionals recognized homosexuals as members of a psychologically healthy minority that share a particular sexual lifestyle, they legitimized the homosexual alternative, purged it officially of the taint of pathology, and enabled homosexual preferences to become the basis for positive group and personal identity.

In the wake of the sexual experimentation that characterized the late 1960s and 1970s, mental-health professionals treated as psychologically normal several nonprocreative sexual options, including mate swapping, masturbation, recreational sex, bisexuality, and homosexuality (Levine and

Troiden 1986). If anything, psychiatrists and allied specialists in sexuality defined "not enough" sex as a psychological problem. Anorgasmia (not having orgasms), inhibited sexual desire (not wanting sex "often enough"), and erectile insufficiency (the inability to have or maintain erections) were defined as sexual dysfunctions, clinical conditions amenable to therapeutic interventions (Edwards 1986; Kaplan 1985; Masters and Johnson 1970). Masturbation, a nonprocreative option, became a respectable strategy for professional treatment of anorgasmia.

Against a sexually permissive backdrop, the focus of homosexuality research changed. Concerns of etiology and treatment were abandoned for preoccupation with the subjective experience of being homosexual in contemporary Western society. In the context of community, culture, relationships, and politics, homosexuality and the issues of group and personal identity emerged as salient research concerns. In particular, homosexual identity formation commanded the attention of social scientists.

Transformation and change were also essential components of the homosexual identity formation models that were discussed in Chapter 4. All models described homosexual identity formation as a protracted process consisting of several stages. When people label themselves as homosexual, they experience an identity transformation, a change in self-perceived sexual orientation from heterosexual or bisexual to homosexual. Like other identities, the homosexual identity is also emergent; it is never determined fully, but is subject to modification and change across the life span. As Chapter 4 showed, the meanings attributed to the homosexual identity, and the significance and centrality of homosexuality, vary over time and place; so do the strategies used to evade or confront the homosexual stigma.

Homosexuality as Health Threat

By the late 1970s, many people felt that sexual liberation had gone too far and that sexual expression had become too far removed from love and commitment. Dissatisfaction with the self-fulfillment ethic led people to adopt what Yankelovich (1984) has termed an "ethic of commitment," which abandons sexual self-interest. Relational and procreative sexual patterns replaced recreational arrangements. Dating, courtship, marriage, and parenthood began to structure sexual interactions; obligations, fidelity, and romance became priorities (Levine and Troiden 1986).

The rise of a politically powerful, well-organized, and heavily financed Christian right — the Moral Majority, Citizens for Decency, and "pro-life" groups — also contributed to the demise of a sexually permissive standard. In combination these groups contributed to a climate that fostered the idea that sex outside of committed, monogamous relationships is dangerous.

These groups have a clear goal: a return to the traditional moral and sexual order, a world devoid of abortion, contraception, pornography, sex education in the schools, premarital sex, and sexual minorities (Levine and Troiden 1986).

The emergence of incurable sexually transmitted diseases — genital herpes, hepatitis B, and AIDS — added support to the conservative attitude toward sex. As a result of the genital herpes and AIDS epidemics, homosexuals and heterosexuals altered their sexual habits. A recent study ("Partners and Practices Changing" 1986) found that in response to the AIDS crisis, a significant majority of gay males have discontinued sex with anonymous partners, have reduced the number of their sexual partners, have adopted "safe sex" practices involving no exchange of bodily fluids, or have entered into monogamous relationships.

The AIDS epidemic poses real threats to the civil liberties of sexual minorities. Historically, dominant groups have used the fear of disease to justify controlling the behavior of subordinate groups (Adam 1978a). In 1918, for example, concern over gonorrhea and syphilis moved the U.S. Congress to enact legislation to establish reformatories in which to detain, isolate, and quarantine infected individuals. More than 18,000 women with sexually transmitted diseases were arrested and locked up in institutions (Brandt 1985).

Because of the high incidence of AIDS among gay males, heterosexual prostitutes, and intravenous drug users (politically subordinate groups), some members of the conservative right have called for a quarantine of people with AIDS and those with antibodies to the AIDS virus. The quarantine argument, however, is undermined by the prohibitive costs of mass AIDS antibody testing, the high rate of false positive reactions to the ELISA test and the need for a repeat test in six months to validate the results (Carter 1986), the association between AIDS and intimate contact (with an exchange of blood or semen) rather than casual contact, and evidence that gay men have modified their sexual habits in the face of the AIDS crisis ("More Gay Men Choosing Celibacy" 1987).

A Return to Etiology

The conservative sexual climate of the late 1970s and early 1980s saw a resurgence of interest in explaining the etiology of homosexuality. A search began for childhood predictors of adult homosexuality. These studies, discussed in Chapter 7, argued that homosexuals exist in all societies and that in any culture, childhood cross-gender behavior occurs more frequently in "prehomosexuals" than in "preheterosexuals." On the basis of these results, the investigators argued that homosexuality is a natural variation, and cited biological factors as the probable causes of both gender behavior and adult sexual preference. Methodological flaws and contradictory results, however, were revealed by critical examinations of the studies that claimed to demonstrate a biological basis for sexual preference. The biological variables responsible for the genesis of sexual preference have not been isolated, if in fact they exist. In addition, although sizable minorities of lesbians and gay males behaved in cross-gendered ways as children, a majority exhibited gender-neutral or gender-appropriate interests and behavior.

Even if gender behavior ("masculinity" and "femininity") and sexual preferences were determined completely by biology, current cultural scenarios would organize and define the meanings of sexuality and gender; the significance of gender behavior and interests; the forms that gender and sexuality should assume, their value, the places where they should occur, and their goals or purposes. Whether a person's place on a Kinsey-like scale of sexual responsiveness and behavior is determined by psychological, social, or biological factors, or by all three, "the homosexual" is constructed to the extent that position on a spectrum provides the basis for such a classification. This construction transforms a matter of degree into one of kind, recasting a form of social behavior into an essential form of being.

Appendix: THE RISKS OF SEX EDUCATION
AND RESEARCH

As Gagnon and Simon (1973) have noted, American cultural messages about sexuality are mixed. Sexuality is presented variously as a sacred act, a form of recreation, a private behavior, something "dirty," a reproductive necessity, a means of intimate expression, a biological drive, or a primitive and mysterious force. Sexuality is both fascinating and frightening, and existing sociocultural arrangements and clandestine learning structures have fostered ambivalent attitudes toward sexuality among Americans.

In the popular mind, the scientific study of sexuality is faintly immoral, even unnatural. By extension, students of sexuality are looked upon as unnaturally interested in sex, and thus sexually suspect:

> Sex research has an irregular history. Much of this is due to the fact that sex has been a stigmatized subject. Proper people simply did not talk or write about it, and, especially, they did not do research about it during the 19th and first part of the 20th centuries. (Bullough 1985, 375)

A preliminary analysis of questionnaires administered to approximately 1000 members of the Society for the Scientific Study of Sex (SSSS) revealed that 32 percent of its members had experienced occupationally related discrimination. The degree of discrimination ranged from

> being the object of snickers and brunt of jokes to being subjected to public demonstrations, ostracism (including ostracism of their families), as well as losing jobs and referrals, and being denied raises and promotions. ("Sexuality Professionals" 1985, 1).

The ambivalent responses to some sexuality experts from other professionals and from the lay public support the assertion that human sexuality is a stigmatizing line of work.

Occupational stigmatization renders sexuality educators and researchers socially marked or markable, depending on context. Professionally, the status of the sexuality educator or researcher is readily apparent, broadcast

130

by topics of research and instruction. Personally, the sexuality expert has greater latitude for disclosing or disguising his or her occupational status. As I demonstrate in this Appendix, some people hold sexuality specialists accountable for their own stigmatization because it stems from or may influence their choice of occupation. Others perceive sex experts as threats to the traditional sexual order or as security risks (Bullough 1985).

Personal Risks

The general public's personal and professional responses to sexuality professionals reflects ambivalent attitudes toward sexuality and uncertainty about what these professionals do. The stigmatizing aspects of careers in sex research and education are probably most visible in the personal realm; personal stigmatization may occur in casual encounters and close (intimate) relations. Personal risks stem from the stereotyped expectations held by members of the wider culture regarding the characteristics of sexuality experts. Jones et al. (1984) define stereotypes as "overgeneralized, largely false beliefs about members of social categories that are frequently, *but not always,* negative" (p. 154; italics added).

In casual encounters, nonspecialists typically learn that individuals are sexuality educators or researchers when they are first introduced. Stereotyped expectations cast sexuality professionals into several possible molds: as questioning the unquestionable, having multiple flaws, sexually unusual, unworthy of belief, undermining traditional values, or advocating the practices investigated.

Questioning the Unquestionable

Some social audiences view sex education and research as attempts at questioning the unquestionable, making a concerted effort to challenge a sexual order that they believe is based either in nature or in that which is sacred. The theme of sexuality professionals as questioners of the unquestionable is revealed in responses such as "How can you do something so gross for a living?" or "Isn't anything sacred to you?" or "You know, there's more to life than just sex." Sexuality specialists are seen as violating a norm that almost everyone else follows: unquestioning acceptance of the existing sexual order. In these cases, the "sexually suspect" stigma is viewed as voluntarily acquired, a consequence of occupational choice.

Having Multiple Flaws

Sometimes audiences react to the knowledge that individuals are sexuality educators and researchers by adding a wide variety of flaws to the original occupational stigma. This process is reflected in such responses as "Isn't it true that many people who do sex research are themselves psychologically disturbed?"; "I've heard that sexual dysfunction is more common among sex therapists and counselors than in the population at large"; "I know of a couple who researched sex, but their marriage was highly unstable"; "People who study sex are the ultimate spectators, afraid to experience their own sexuality"; or (at a sexuality workshop) "I wonder how many people here are taking this workshop to resolve their own sexual problems?" In these cases the "sexually suspect" stigma is attributed to developmental flaws such as an obsessive interest in, or fear of, sex.

Occupying Sexual Extremes

A third stereotyped response to sexuality specialists is to characterize them as occupying sexual extremes, possessing a number of positive or negative attributes, depending on perspective. Extreme level of sexual desire is one expectation: "I'll bet you can't get it often enough." Extreme sexual prowess is another, as expressed by the statement "I bet you're something else in bed." Other people assume that the sexuality specialist possesses vast sexual experience. The comment "I'll bet you've tried it all" reflects this expectation. Sexual specialization is yet another presumption: "What kink are you into?" A few people see sex experts as exhibiting all of these extremes. In such cases, sexuality specialists are seen as promiscuous savages, ever on the prowl for sex and driven by the need for sexual variety, improved technique, novelty, and orgasmic release.

At other times, audience expectations regarding sexuality specialists are more positive. Sexuality professionals are sometimes assumed to possess high levels of sexual health. The comments "You seem so together about sex" or "You've done a remarkable job of integrating your sexuality into your personality" reflect these expectations. Finally, sexuality professionals are sometimes looked upon as sexual gurus, possessed of limitless sexual lore, capable of diagnosing and resolving sexual concerns with a few well-chosen words and specific suggestions.

Unworthy of Belief

Disbelief is another audience response to the sexuality educator or researcher. Individuals sometimes refuse to honor professionals' claims to being sex researchers or educators, and treat such claims as jokes or attempts at humor. At other times, disbelief stems from the assumption that sexual knowledge is acquired naturally: "Who'd ever think there'd come a time when people would have to be taught about sex or take classes to learn how to have a baby?" In these instances, sexologists' activities are trivialized; they and their work become the objects of snickers and the brunt of jokes.

Sources of Peril

In another audience response to sexuality professionals, a theory or ideology is constructed to explain their disvalued status and to account for the danger it represents. In these instances, the perils and the historical-precedent dimensions of stigma come heavily into play. Members of highly conservative religious groups frequently cast sexuality professionals into the role of "godless secular humanists" set on altering or destroying America's most cherished family values. A female student, for example, recently accused me of "not loving our Lord" because I stated that, according to research, homosexuality poses few, if any, threats to traditional family life (AIDS notwithstanding).

Sexuality educators are especially vulnerable to the charge of subverting traditional family values. They are often perceived as influencing their students powerfully by exposing them to potentially harmful (i.e., liberal) attitudes toward sexuality. Jones et al. (1984) made a similar point when they discussed public perceptions of ex-mental patients:

> Since the more power someone has, the more harm that person can do, it seems likely that society will be very reluctant to assign mentally questionable people to positions of power and that candidates for important jobs will be carefully screened to be certain that they are balanced and reliable. (p. 69)

Advocates and Practitioners

Another audience reaction is the presumption that sexuality experts both advocate and practice the sexual patterns they investigate. Thus, homosexuality researchers are presumed to be homosexual, students of nudism are presumed to be nudists, extramarital sex investigators are thought to "swing in wedlock," students of sadomasochism are believed to be devotees, and so forth. As researchers' topics change, so may the expectations surrounding their alleged sexual interests and practices. One expert, who initially researched homosexuality, has recently investigated heterosexual patterns. This change in emphasis apparently altered a colleague's presumptions about the expert's sexual preferences. While lecturing on homosexuality, the colleague used the expert to illustrate how a person's sexual preference may be fluid enough to permit alternation between heterosexual and homosexual patterns. This was a remarkable statement, since the expert had never discussed his sexuality or private life with this colleague.

The stigma attaching to sex research may continue to plague a researcher even after his or her research interests have evolved in directions considered more conventional. One woman, who conducted a landmark study of extramarital sex, recently developed an interest in examining the relatively uncontroversial topic of adult sibling relationships. Her past record as a sex researcher, however, led some of her colleagues to presume that brother/sister incest was the topic of her latest investigations.

Sexuality experts' intimate partners may also harbor ambivalent expectations. They may expect specialists to be "super lovers"—totally attentive, uninhibited mistresses or masters of erotic technique. They may assume that the professionals expect them to be "wanton" and "wild," which may promote "performance anxiety." At other times, partners may fear that sexuality professionals view sex as an analytical exercise or an applied experiment, and may say, "Are you sure you don't analyze and evaluate everything we do sexually?" Alternatively, intimate partners may fear that specialists prefer the sexual patterns they are investigating to those in which the couple indulge together ("Are you sure prostitutes aren't more exciting to you?").

Variables Related to Risks

As the SSSS membership poll indicated, sexuality experts are not stigmatized uniformly. Two-thirds of the SSSS members did not report having experienced occupational discrimination, but the preliminary data analysis has yet to report variables that may explain the reported differences in stigmatization.

Social Factors

My observations of and discussions with other sexuality specialists suggest that a number of social, personal, and audience variables may affect the level of stigmatization encountered. A sex expert's social attributes seem to influence audience perceptions of him or her as a person; age, sex, appearance, marital status, and family status may guide and mold these perceptions. Singles appear more vulnerable to marking than married persons. Similarly, older, married, less physically attractive sex specialists appear to encounter less stigmatization than younger, single, more physically attractive professionals. Women — especially young, attractive women — seem to be stigmatized more readily than men. Married couples with families may appear more conventional in the eyes of the public than married, childless couples, and thus may encounter less stigmatization.

Along these lines, Dr. Ruth Westheimer's popularity may be attributed in part to the fact that, knowingly or unknowingly, she fits many of the wider culture's stereotypes of both aged persons and sexuality specialists. She is maternal, the "mother" we can talk to about sex. She is direct, outspoken, even outrageous — all prerogatives permitted a woman of her age. She is also obviously sexual and willing to spice up a sexual relationship with practices that some people might consider unconventional.

Personal Factors

On the personal level, audience perceptions of sex experts seem to be influenced by the kinds of intimate relationships they think the experts have. Some close relationships are more susceptible to marking than others: Same-sex couples seem more markable than heterosexual cohabitors, who in turn seem more suspect than traditional married couples. Audience concepts of a sexuality specialist's sexual preferences are also important: An expert perceived as homosexual or bisexual appears to be at greater risk of stigmatization than one presumed to be heterosexual.

Audience Factors

Audience characteristics may also increase or decrease the likelihood of stigmatization. Jones et al. (1984) noted that social class affects attributions of deviance in general and mental illness in particular. The higher an individual's social class, the more likely he or she is to make attributions of deviance. Social distance between markers and marked also influences the probability of marking: the greater the distance, the greater the likelihood of stigmatization. Jones et al. (1984) identified two components of social distance, *relational distance* and *cultural distance:*

> Relational distance means the degree of interpersonal involvement between people, as indicated by such things as the scope, frequency, length, and intensity of their interactions. By this definition, an individual's family and kin are at the closest relational distance, followed by friends, neighbors, acquaintances, and then strangers. Cultural distance [is] the extent to which individuals share such characteristics as ethnicity, social class, and religion. (p. 107)

Typically, people relationally close to marked individuals deny or "normalize" the stigma, whereas those at greater relational distances are more likely to perceive the stigma negatively. The same pattern is evident in cultural distance; greater distance is linked with greater stigmatization.

Biological sex and professional status are also related to a general willingness to stigmatize. Women are more apt to impute deviance than men (Jones et al. 1984); professionals are more likely to make deviance designations than nonprofessionals (Lofland 1969). More research is needed to isolate various combinations of audience and actor characteristics that explain different levels of stigmatization of sexuality experts.

Professional Risks

The public image of sexologists as sexually suspect provides a backdrop against which nonsexuality specialists assess and judge the professional contributions of sex experts in academic settings. The presumption that sexuality specialists are sexually unconventional may affect the way in which administrators evaluate research and writing on sexual issues, and their willingness to support such endeavors. Professionals who lack training in relativizing disciplines, such as sociology, psychology, and anthropology, may see deviance and conformity as invariant, internal properties rather than outcomes of culturally and situationally created labeling; thus they lack the training necessary for objective assessment of controversial research and theorizing.

The professional risks encountered by sexuality specialists in academic settings may be traced to several sources: the multidisciplinary approach to sex; the highly specialized nature of sex research; the potential peril; the intrinsic interest of the subject; the controversial course content and advising; the use of instructional audiovisuals; and the expectations of student audiences.

A Multidisciplinary Field

The multidisciplinary nature of sex research and education usually necessitates publishing in multidisciplinary journals. Publishing in journals outside the major discipline may place academic sexuality experts at professional risk within their major discipline if their department, division, or college places a higher value on works published in mainstream journals within the major discipline than on those appearing in multidisciplinary publications. The multidisciplinary nature of sexuality research may also make it more difficult to locate people within the major discipline to serve as outside reviewers of research papers on sexuality.

Specialization

Sexuality research is also highly specialized, which may generate the charge of overspecialization. One dean recently informed a sexuality professional that although his sexuality research was important, he had carved out such a specialized niche that it limited his chances of developing a national reputation in the major discipline — an institutional requirement for promotion.

Potential Peril

From an administrative perspective, the possible peril of including sexuality professionals on the staff may outweigh the perceived benefits. For this reason, the sexual topics that individuals investigate may affect their initial chances of obtaining a position or the ease of moving from one position to another. When one sexuality expert first applied for a job, his vita informed prospective employers of his research on homosexuality. This individual had applied only to universities that expressed an interest in hiring a "deviance" specialist, but most of these institutions did not acknowledge receipt of the application or inform the applicant that he was being considered for the job. At one university the candidate's name was withdrawn from the candidate pool after a formal interview because, according to one member of the search committee, the administration felt uncomfortable about affiliating a homosexuality researcher with their institution.

Specialized research interests may similarly limit the chances to move from one university to another. One nationally recognized sex researcher received unsolicited job offers from other universities until he undertook research on homosexuality. From that point on, the number of offers declined noticeably.

Intrinsic Interest

The intrinsic interest that sexuality and sex research hold for professionals and the lay public may also provide grounds for discounting excellent teaching evaluations in sexuality and sex-related courses. During the spring 1985 semester, for example, I received an award for outstanding teaching. This award had not been offered in eleven years; seven hundred people were eligible; eighty were nominated; and four received the award. On hearing the news of the award, a colleague from another discipline remarked casually, "Well, what do you expect? You teach sex," as if the topic alone guaranteed excellent evaluations.

Controversial Course Content

Many topics covered routinely in human sexuality classes are controversial, creating yet another source of risk. The potential for conflict is
always present when classroom lectures and discussions routinely address
abortion, homosexuality, sadomasochism, masturbation, pornography,
extramarital sex, and contraception (McKinney 1985). Instructors are often
accused of advocacy when they present information challenging the alleged
pathology of controversial activities, and in this sense they may be perceived
as sources of peril.

One sexuality specialist who discussed nonsexist childrearing practices
with her class acknowledged that she did not discourage her son from playing with dolls. She was shocked to learn that a deputation of students approached her department chair to determine if the courts could gain
custody of her son for "his own good." Her department chair requested that
in the future she refrain from discussing her childrearing practices in class.
Instructors who find themselves embroiled in controversies stemming from
course topics run the risk of being defined institutionally as "trouble-
makers," sources of peril, or poor risks for tenure and promotion, especially
when the controversy spills out of the classroom and into the wider community.

Controversial Advising

Sexuality specialists may also incur professional risk because of their
willingness to serve as faculty advisors to controversial student groups. A
gay campus organization, for example, recently approached a female sexuality
specialist and asked her to advise them. When the instructor discussed this
request with her department chair, the chair was appalled, and claimed that
her chances of obtaining tenure might be jeopardized if she advised the
group. Nonetheless, she agreed to act as advisor. (She did not gain tenure
because of the "overly political and rhetorical nature" of her work.)

Use of Audiovisuals

Classroom use of sexually explicit materials may also generate levels of
controversy that the untenured neophyte may wish to avoid, especially
when the conflict mobilizes community-interest groups. Recently an
untenured professor showed a college sexuality class an X-rated movie to
demonstrate how pornography distorts expectations about the nature of
male and female sexuality. Attendance was voluntary, and relevant ad-

ministrators were informed in advance about the time, date, and purpose of the film. A local community group got wind of the project and staged an antipornography demonstration. In this case, the university administration backed the instructor solidly because it places strong emphasis on academic freedom.

In another instance, a first-year, untenured faculty member showed his sexuality class films about homosexual lovemaking to underscore the similarity between heterosexual and homosexual patterns. One student, offended by the sexually explicit nature of the films, complained to the instructor's department chair. The chair met with the instructor and expressed his displeasure over the use of such films in class, and ended the conversation with the statement, "I won't have you advocating homosexuality in the classroom." Another department chair regarded a sexuality specialist as promoting premarital sex because she showed her sexuality classes films dealing with heterosexual lovemaking.

A departmental chair who supports an individual's decision to show sexually explicit films in his or her classes provides an important source of faculty morale. One department chair considered previewing all films shown in human sexuality classes but decided against such a move; he reasoned that such a policy would be discriminatory because he did not preview films shown in other courses. This chair also felt that the instructor was in a better position to judge what kinds of sexuality films would be appropriate for the class.

Student Expectations

Student expectations may also create problems for human sexuality instructors (McKinney 1985). Some students assume that they will excel in class because of the vastness of their sexual experiences. These students may be upset when confronted by demanding examinations on multidisciplinary course content rather than on sexual experience and technique. Other students become distressed when instructors refuse to endorse or condemn certain sexual patterns (e.g., premarital sex or homosexuality), and stress instead the importance of active decision making, choices, consequences, self-responsibility, and acting in accordance with deeply held values. Disenchanted students may occasionally retaliate by complaining to the departmental chair and by giving instructors low ratings in course evaluations.

Professional Reactions

After they encounter people with stigmatizing expectations, sexuality professionals may experience increasingly ambivalent attitudes about interacting with nonspecialists. They may become unsure of how others will react to them, or wonder what more conventional people really think of them. This awareness may make specialists feel as if they are "on stage," self-aware and calculating, and careful about the impressions they make both inside and outside work. In other cases, sexuality professionals may feel (and fear) that the accomplishments they see as minor will be regarded by nonspecialists as remarkable or noteworthy. Some colleagues, for example, find it amazing that sex educators and researchers can discuss sensitive sexual topics comfortably in large classes attended by students of both sexes. At still other times, sexuality professionals may fear that minor failings may be seen as growing out of the disvalued status. A department chair, for example, may perceive a sexuality expert's occasional lack of punctuality as evidence of a "sexually irresponsible" attitude. The ambivalence that sexuality specialists feel toward nonspecialists may be managed through situational strategies, withdrawal, or redefinition.

Situational Strategies

Goffman (1963) and Jones et al. (1984) suggest that stigmatized persons react to stereotypic expectations in a number of ways. In the context of sexuality, one obvious response is to leave the field, to stop conducting sexuality research or teaching sexuality classes. One sexuality educator stopped teaching sex courses because the topics covered contain the potential for conflict and strife. Yet another colleague switched the focus of her research when her dean stated, "We don't like sex at this university." Another response involves selective self-disclosure—a general unwillingness to broadcast topics of one's research or teaching with nonintimates (Troiden 1981; Weinberg and Williams 1972). I sometimes tell strangers that I study identity or teach social studies simply because I am tired of explaining and justifying my research and teaching.

Other sexuality experts respond to the stigma by saying or doing nothing in class that is not supported by the literature. Still other specialists may react by using the stigma of sexuality for the secondary gains it provides, such as excuses (justified or not) for failure or a general lack of success: "I would have been promoted [or tenured] if I had avoided research and teaching in the area of sex."

Withdrawal

The "sexually suspect" stigma surrounding the status of sexuality educator or researcher may also set sexuality professionals apart from society and sometimes from themselves. They may feel discredited socially, nearly alone occupationally, at the fringes of an unaccepting world. As a result, some sexuality experts may confine their interactions to their "own"—those similarly stigmatized—and to the "wise"—sympathetic outsiders who honor claims to equal treatment—who are perceived as sources of support and reassurance. Withdrawal into a community of like-situated others has important implications for the self-esteem of sexuality professionals:

> Exposure to others with similar problems has at least two important consequences. It allows for comparison with respect to coping with the stigma. Second, comparison with people who are similarly marked or stigmatized should allow individuals to focus on attributes and qualities other than the stigmatized ones, and thereby provide the opportunity for them to view themselves as complex and differentiated individuals with valued attributes and abilities. (Jones et al. 1984, 144)

Redefinition

The stigmatizing features of a career in sexuality may be viewed alternatively as a blessing in disguise, creating greater self-awareness, strength of character, or sexual integration. Most of the sexuality specialists I know fall into this category. The SSSS study cited earlier verifies my observations: 68 percent of the SSSS members reported feeling positive about their choice of profession ("Sexuality Professionals" 1985). In a more defensive spirit, sex experts may respond by cataloging the sexual failings of other professionals; they may point out that on balance, the general population possesses the sexual problem, not the sexuality specialists.

Academic Factors and Stigmatization

Personal and social characteristics are not the only possible reasons for differences in the stigmatization of sexuality educators and researchers. Stigmatization may also be explained by social-structural variables, especially an individual's professional status, the prevailing economic climate, the immediate work environment, and institutional goals.

Professional Status

Sexuality educators who have achieved relatively high levels of professional status within their disciplines and work settings appear less vulnerable to stigmatization than those who rank lower. Professional status reflects the individual's level of power, which is the ability to mobilize support for activities. Several factors determine an individual's power. Excellence in teaching, as measured by standardized evaluation forms, is one. Another is high-quality research, as measured by the number and type of publications. A third is university service, as measured by roles on key university committees. Yet another factor is tenure, which tends to be granted only to those who show promise in teaching, research, and service. Other factors that increase power are the ability to obtain research grants; the size, number, type (graduate or undergraduate), and demand for courses taught; and professional prestige and service within the discipline. A track record of professional excellence may lead administrators to conclude that the benefits of having a nationally prominent sexuality expert on the faculty outweigh the potential liabilities.

Economic Climate

Economic climate, as part of the wider culture, may also play a role in the stigmatization of sexuality professionals. Jones et al. (1984) note that economic downswings decrease public tolerance of stigma, whereas economic upswings increase tolerance. The economic downswings of the late 1970s and early 1980s may partly explain the public's increased concern over the topics addressed in sex-education courses. Along these lines, Francoeur (1982) argues that the range of sexual behaviors perceived as deviant or immoral increases during economic downswings; at those times conservative movements emerge to advocate a return to traditional family values. This assertion is supported by the recent emergence of conservative or fundamentalist religious groups.

Immediate Work Environment

The immediate work environment also influences the level of stigmatization. The social distance between sexuality specialists and those who judge their contributions seems important. When academic deans and chairs are relationally and culturally close to sexuality specialists, stigmatization appears to be lowest. Such closeness occurs when all parties interact regularly and value responsibly conducted research and teaching, and when administrators at all levels are willing to champion professionally active and involved colleagues. Supportive colleagues, especially senior colleagues, are also important. Endorsement and support from administrators and colleagues appear to reduce greatly the level of professional stigmatization in academic settings.

Institutional Goals

Institutional goals are also important. Professional stigmatization appears to be greatest in private or denominational academic settings, where the topics or the approach of sex research and education are perceived as threatening or undermining officially stated goals (e.g., developing "Christian character" or "Christian morality"). Universities that stress the importance of academic freedom and value pluralism seem to provide a more supportive professional environment for sexologists. Sexuality specialists are represented disproportionately in public universities; this phenomenon may account for the response by 96 percent of the SSSS members polled, who felt that their professional standings had been enhanced as a result of their sexuality-related work ("Sexuality Professionals" 1985).

Why Remain? A Personal View

Given the risks, why does a professional remain in the field of sexuality? First, the subject matter is interesting. Sex is fascinating to the specialist and the general public alike. Keeping up on the literature is more a joy than a chore, a source of fascination rather than boredom. Second, teaching sexuality provides an opportunity to dispel sexual misinformation, to replace myth with fact. Eliminating ignorance is gratifying. Third, a pluralistic approach to sexuality provides a platform for discussing the dangers posed by conservative attempts to impose a moral hegemony on American society. A spirited defense of value pluralism is not without its pleasures.

The renown and popularity of human sexuality courses may also gratify the ego. After all, an instructor seldom has the opportunity to be a "star," forced to turn away hundreds from an already packed house. In addition, sexuality research is still in its adolescence. A scholar can conduct pathfinding research and form fresh theories, especially on variant sexualities. Research at the edge of a "forbidden frontier" is appealing on several levels. Also, I would argue that a researcher should not allow the dictates of conventional morality to determine what should or should not be investigated. Yielding to these pressures limits the scope of research to topics considered politically and socially "correct" by the mainstream and relegates social-science research to the study of etiquette.

Studying and teaching human sexuality may also be a liberating occasion for personal growth. Instructors must often overcome their own inhibitions to be comfortable in teaching a course on such delicate topics. Finally, professional involvement provides the opportunity to meet fellow travelers, sources of inspiration and support as well as knowledge. As Goffman (1963) would have predicted, I conclude by saying that managing the stigma of the sexually suspect has made me a better person.

REFERENCES

Adam, Barry D. 1978a. *The Survival of Domination.* New York: Elsevier.
_____. 1978b. "Inferiorization and Self-Esteem." *Social Psychology* 41(1): 47–53.
_____. 1985. "Age, Structure, and Sexuality: Reflections on the Anthropological Evidence on Homosexual Relations." *Journal of Homosexuality* 11(3/4): 19–33.
Allport, Gordon W. 1961. *Pattern and Growth in Personality.* New York: Holt, Rinehart, & Winston.
Altman, Dennis. 1971. *Homosexual: Oppression and Liberation.* New York: Outerbridge & Dienstfrey.
_____. 1982. *The Homosexualization of America.* New York: St. Martin's Press.
Anjzen, Icek, and Martin Fishbein. 1973. "Attitudinal and Normative Variables as Predictors of Specific Behaviors." *Journal of Personality and Social Psychology* 27(1): 41–57.
Atchley, Robert C. 1982. "The Aging Self." *Psychotherapy: Theory, Research, and Practice* 19(4): 388–96.
Becker, Howard S. 1963. *Outsiders: Studies in the Sociology of Deviance.* Glencoe, Ill.: Free Press.
Bell, Alan P. 1982. "Sexual Preference: A Postscript." *SIECUS Report* 11(2): 1–3.
Bell, Alan P., and Martin S. Weinberg. 1978. *Homosexualities: A Study of Diversity among Men and Women.* New York: Simon & Schuster.
Bell, Alan P., Martin S. Weinberg, and Sue Kiefer Hammersmith. 1981a. *Sexual Preference: Its Development in Men and Women.* Bloomington: Indiana University Press.
_____. 1981b. *Sexual Preference: Its Development in Men and Women: Statistical Appendix.* Bloomington: Indiana University Press.
Bieber, Irving, Harvey J. Dain, Paul R. Dince, Marvin G. Drellich, Henry G. Grand, Ralph H. Gundlach, Malvina W. Kremer, Alfred H. Rifkin, Cornelia B. Wilbur, and Toby B. Bieber. 1962. *Homosexuality: A Psychoanalytic Study of Male Homosexuals.* New York: Vintage Books.
Birke, Lynda I. A. 1981. "Is Homosexuality Hormonally Determined?" *Journal of Homosexuality* 6(4): 35–49.
Blackwood, Evelyn. 1985. "Breaking the Mirror: The Construction of Lesbianism and the Anthropological Discourse on Homosexuality." *Journal of Homosexuality* 11(3/4): 1–17.
Blumstein, Philip E., and Pepper Schwartz. 1974. "Lesbianism and Bisexuality." In *Sexual Deviance and Sexual Deviants,* edited by Erich Goode and Richard R. Troiden, 278–95. New York: Morrow.
_____. 1977. "Bisexuality: Some Social-Psychological Issues." *Journal of Social Issues* 33(2): 30–45.
_____. 1983. *American Couples.* New York: Morrow.
Brandt, Allan M. 1985. *No Magic Bullet: A Social History of Venereal Disease in the U.S.* New York: Oxford University Press.
Brim, Orville G., Jr. 1960. "Personality Development as Role Learning." In *Personality Development in Children,* edited by Ira Iscoe and Harold W. Stevenson, 127–59. Austin: University of Texas Press.

144

Brownfain, John J. 1985. "A Study of the Married Bisexual Male: Paradox and Resolution." *Journal of Homosexuality* 11(1/2): 173-88.

Bullough, Vern L. 1985. "Problems of Research on a Delicate Topic: A Personal View." *Journal of Sex Research* 21(4): 375-86.

Burke, Kenneth. 1945. *A Grammar of Motives.* New York: Prentice-Hall.

Califia, Pat. 1979. "Lesbian Sexuality." *Journal of Homosexuality* 4(3): 255-66.

Carrier, Joseph M. 1975. "Comments on 'A Neuroendocrine Predisposition for Homosexuality in Men.'" *Archives of Sexual Behavior* 4(6): 667.

Carter, D. Bruce. 1986. "AIDS and the Sex Therapist: 'Just the Facts Please, Ma'am.'" *Journal of Sex Research* 22(3): 403-8.

Cass, Vivienne C. 1979. "Homosexual Identity Formation: A Theoretical Model." *Journal of Homosexuality* 4(3): 219-35.

_____. 1983/1984. "Homosexual Identity: A Concept in Need of Definition." *Journal of Homosexuality* 9(2/3): 105-26.

_____. 1984. "Homosexual Identity Formation: Testing a Theoretical Model." *Journal of Sex Research* 20(2): 143-67.

Chesebro, James W. 1981. "Views of Homosexuality among Social Scientists." In *Gay Speak: Gay Male and Lesbian Communication,* edited by James W. Chesebro, 175-88. New York: Pilgrim Press.

Coleman, Eli. 1982. "Developmental Stages of the Coming-Out Process." In *Homosexuality: Social, Psychological, and Biological Issues,* edited by William Paul, James D. Weinrich, John C. Gonsiorek, and Mary E. Hotvedt, 149-58. Beverly Hills: Sage.

_____. 1985a. "Bisexual Women in Marriages." *Journal of Homosexuality* 11(1/2): 87-99.

_____. 1985b. "Integration of Male Bisexuality and Marriage." *Journal of Homosexuality* 11(1/2): 189-207.

Cooley, Charles H. 1902. *Human Nature and the Social Order.* New York: Scribner's.

Corbett, Sherry L., Richard R. Troiden, and Richard A. Dodder. 1974. "Tolerance as a Correlate of Experience with Stigma: The Case of the Homosexual." *Journal of Homosexuality* 3(1): 3-13.

Cressey, Donald R. 1953. *Other People's Money.* Glencoe, Ill.: Free Press.

Cronin, Denise M. 1974. "Coming Out among Lesbians." In *Sexual Deviance and Sexual Deviants,* edited by Erich Goode and Richard R. Troiden, 268-77. New York: Morrow.

Dank, Barry M. 1971. "Coming Out in the Gay World." *Psychiatry* 34(2): 180-97.

_____. 1972. "Why Homosexuals Marry Heterosexual Women." *Medical Aspects of Human Sexuality* 6(August): 14-23.

Davies, Nigel. 1984. *The Rampant God: Eros throughout the World.* New York: Morrow.

Davis, Alan J. 1972. "Sexual Assaults in the Philadelphia Prison System." In *Muckraking Sociology,* edited by Gary T. Marx, 31-39. New Brunswick, N.J.: Transaction Books.

De Cecco, John P. 1987. "Homosexuality's Brief Recovery: From Sickness to Health and Back Again." *Journal of Sex Research* 23(1): 106-114.

DeLamater, John. 1981. "The Social Control of Sexuality." *Annual Review of Sociology* 7: 263-90.

Delph, Edward. 1979. *The Silent Community.* Beverly Hills: Sage.

de Monteflores, Carmen, and Stephen J. Schultz. 1978. "Coming Out: Similarities and Differences for Lesbians and Gay Men." *Journal of Social Issues* 34(3): 59-72.

Dörner, Gunter. 1976. *Hormones and Brain Differentiation.* Amsterdam: Elsevier.

_____. 1977. "Sex-Hormone-Dependent Brain Differentiation and Reproduction." In *Handbook of Sexology,* edited by John Money and Herman Musaph, 227–43. New York: Elsevier.

Dörner, Gunter, Wolfgang Rohde, Fritz Stahl, Lothar Krell, and Wolf-Günther Masius. 1975. "A Neuroendocrine Predisposition for Homosexuality in Men." *Archives of Sexual Behavior* 4(1): 1–8.

Dover, Kenneth J. 1978. *Greek Homosexuality.* New York: Vintage Books.

Doyle, James A. 1983. *The Male Experience.* Dubuque, Iowa: Wm. C. Brown.

Edwards, Sharon. 1986. "A Sex Addict Speaks." *SIECUS Report* 14(6): 1–3.

Ehrhardt, Anke A., Kathryn Evers, and John Money. 1968. "Influence of Androgen and Some Aspects of Sexual Dimorphic Behavior in Women with the Late-Treated Adrenogenital Syndrome." *Johns Hopkins Medical Journal* 123: 115–22.

Erikson, Erik. 1959. "Identity and the Life-Cycle." *Psychological Issues* 1(1): 1–171.

Evans, Ray B. 1970. "Sixteen Personality Factor Questionnaire Scores of Homosexual Men." *Journal of Consulting and Clinical Psychology* 34(2): 212–15.

Faderman, Lillian. 1981. *Surpassing the Love of Men: Romantic Friendship and Love Patterns between Women from the Renaissance to the Present.* London: Junction Books.

_____. 1984/1985. "The 'New Gay' Lesbians." *Journal of Homosexuality* 10(3/4): 85–95.

Foucault, Michel. 1979. *The History of Sexuality. Volume 1, An Introduction.* London: Allen Lane.

Forsyth, Craig, and Robert Gramling. 1986. "Expanding a Typology of the Dimensions of Marked Relationships: A Theoretical Note." *Deviant Behavior* 7(1): 47–51.

Francoeur, Robert T. 1982. *Becoming a Sexual Person.* New York: Wiley.

Freedman, Mark. 1971. *Homosexuality and Psychological Functioning.* Belmont, Calif.: Brooks/Cole.

Gagnon, John H. 1977. *Human Sexualities.* Glenview, Ill.: Scott, Foresman.

Gagnon, John H., and William Simon. 1973. *Sexual Conduct: The Social Sources of Human Sexuality.* Chicago: Aldine.

Goffman, Erving. 1959. *The Presentation of Self in Everyday Life.* New York: Basic Books.

_____. 1963. *Stigma: Notes on the Management of Spoiled Identity.* Englewood Cliffs, N.J.: Prentice-Hall.

Goode, Erich. 1973. *The Drug Phenomenon: Social Aspects of Drug Taking.* Indianapolis: Bobbs-Merrill.

_____. 1981a. "Comments on the Homosexual Role." *Journal of Sex Research* 17(1): 54–65.

_____. 1981b. "The Homosexual Role: Rejoinder to Omark and Whitam." *Journal of Sex Research* 17(1): 76–83.

_____. 1984. *Deviant Behavior.* 2d ed. Englewood Cliffs, N.J.: Prentice-Hall.

Goode, Erich, and Richard R. Troiden. 1974. "Male Homosexuality." In *Sexual Deviance and Sexual Deviants,* edited by Erich Goode and Richard R. Troiden, 149–60. New York: Morrow.

Green, Richard. 1972. "Homosexuality as a Mental Illness." *International Journal of Psychiatry* 10(1): 77–98.

_____. 1974. *Sexual Identity Conflict in Children and Adults.* New York: Basic Books.

_____. 1976. "One-Hundred Ten Feminine and Masculine Boys: Behavioral Contrasts and Demographic Similarities." *Archives of Sexual Behavior* 5(5): 425–46.

_____. 1979. "Childhood Cross-Gender Behavior and Subsequent Sexual Preference." *American Journal of Psychiatry* 136(1): 106–8.

_____. 1987. *The "Sissy Boy Syndrome" and the Development of Homosexuality.* New Haven, Conn.: Yale University Press.

Hammersmith, Sue Kiefer, and Martin S. Weinberg. 1973. "Homosexual Identity, Commitment, Adjustments, and Significant Others." *Sociometry* 36(1): 56–78.

Harry, Joseph. 1982. *Gay Children Grown Up: Gender Culture and Gender Deviance.* New York: Praeger.

_____. 1984/1985. "Sexual Orientation as Destiny." *Journal of Homosexuality* 10(3/4): 111–24.

Harry, Joseph, and William DeVall. 1978. *The Social Organization of Gay Males.* New York: Praeger.

Hart, John, and Diane Richardson, eds. 1981. *The Theory and Practice of Homosexuality*. London: Routledge & Kegan Paul.

Heffernan, Esther. 1972. *Making It in Prison: the Square, the Cool, and the Life.* New York: Wiley-Interscience.

Hencken, Joel D., and William T. O'Dowd. 1977. "Coming Out as an Aspect of Identity Formation." *Gai Saber* 1(1): 18–26.

Herdt, Gilbert H. 1981. *Guardians of the Flutes: Idioms of Masculinity.* New York: McGraw-Hill.

Hill, Stuart L. 1980. *Demystifying Social Deviance.* New York: McGraw-Hill.

Hocquenghem, Guy. 1978. *Homosexual Desire.* London: Allison & Busby.

Hoffman, Martin. 1972. "The Male Prostitute." *Sexual Behavior* 2(1): 19–21.

Hooker, Evelyn. 1957. "The Adjustment of the Male Overt Homosexual." *Journal of Projective Techniques* 21(1): 18–31.

_____. 1958. "Male Homosexuality in the Rorschach." *Journal of Projective Techniques* 22(1): 33–54.

Hopkins, June H. 1969. "The Lesbian Personality." *British Journal of Psychiatry* 115: 1433–36.

Hoult, Thomas F. 1983/1984. "Human Sexuality in Biological Perspective: Theoretical and Methodological Considerations." *Journal of Homosexuality* 9(2/3): 137–55.

Humphreys, Laud. 1970. *Tearoom Trade: Impersonal Sex in Public Places.* Chicago: Aldine.

_____. 1972. *Out of the Closets: The Sociology of Homosexual Liberation.* Englewood Cliffs, N.J.: Prentice-Hall.

_____. 1979. "Being Odd against All Odds." In *Sociology,* 2d ed., edited by Ronald C. Federico, 238–42. Reading, Mass.: Addison-Wesley.

Humphreys, Laud, and Brian Miller. 1980. "Identities in the Emerging Gay Culture." In *Homosexual Behavior: A Modern Reappraisal,* edited by Judd Marmor, 142–56. New York: Basic Books.

Hunt, Morton. 1974. *Sexual Behavior in the 1970s.* Chicago: Playboy Press.

James, William. 1892. *Psychology.* New York: Holt.

Jones, Edward E., Amerigo Farina, Albert H. Hastorf, Hazel Markus, Dale T. Miller, and Robert A. Scott. 1984. *Social Stigma: The Psychology of Marked Relationships.* New York: Freeman.

Kaplan, Helen S. 1985. *Comprehensive Evaluation of Disorders of Sexual Desire.* Washington, D.C.: American Psychiatric Press.

Katz, Jack. 1972. "Deviance, Charisma, and Role-Defined Behavior." *Social Problems* 20(2): 186–202.

Kelly, Raymond C. 1976. "Witchcraft and Sexual Relations: An Exploration in the Social and Semantic Implications of a Structure of Belief." In *Man and Woman in the New Guinea Highlands,* edited by Paula Brown and Georgeda Buchbinder, 36–53. Washington, D.C.: American Anthropological Association.

Kinsey, Alfred C., Wardell B. Pomeroy, and Clyde E. Martin. 1948. *Sexual Behavior in the Human Male.* Philadelphia: Saunders.

Kinsey, Alfred C., Wardell B. Pomeroy, Clyde E. Martin, and Paul H. Gebhard. 1953. *Sexual Behavior in the Human Female.* Philadelphia: Saunders.

Klein, Fritz, Barry Sepekoff, and Timothy J. Wolf. 1985. "Sexual Orientation: A Multi-Variable Dynamic Process." *Journal of Homosexuality* 11(1/2): 35–49.

Kooden, Harold D., Stephen F. Morin, Dorothy I. Riddle, Martin Rogers, Barbara E. Strang, and Frank Strassburger. 1979. *Removing the Stigma: Final Report of the Board of Social and Ethical Responsibility for Psychology's Task Force on the Status of Lesbian and Gay Male Psychologists.* Washington, D.C.: American Psychological Association.

Laws, Judith L., and Pepper Schwartz. 1977. *Sexual Scripts: The Social Construction of Female Sexuality.* Hinsdale, Ill.: Dryden Press.

Lee, John Alan. 1977. "Going Public: A Study in the Sociology of Homosexual Liberation." *Journal of Homosexuality* 3(1): 49–78.

_____. 1978. *Getting Sex.* Don Mills, Ontario, Canada: Musson.

Lessard, Suzannah. 1972. "Gay Is Good for Us All." In *The Homosexual Dialectic,* edited by Joseph A. McCaffrey, 205–18. Englewood Cliffs, N.J.: Prentice-Hall.

Levine, Martin P. 1987. "Gay Macho: Ethnography of the Homosexual Clone." Doctoral dissertation, New York University.

Levine, Martin P., and Richard R. Troiden. 1986. "The Sexual Addiction Movement as Moral Crusade." Paper presented at the annual meetings of the American Sociological Association, New York City.

Lindesmith, Alfred R., and Anselm Strauss. 1956. *Social Psychology.* New York: Dryden Press.

Lockard, Denyse. 1985. "The Lesbian Community: An Anthropological Approach." *Journal of Homosexuality* 11(3/4): 83–95.

Lofland, John. 1969. *Deviance and Identity.* Englewood Cliffs, N.J.: Prentice-Hall.

Luker, Kristin. 1984. *Abortion and the Politics of Motherhood.* Berkeley: University of California Press.

Maslow, Abraham H. 1968. "Peak Experiences as Acute Identity-Experiences." In *The Self in Social Interaction,* edited by Chad Gordon and Kenneth J. Gergen, 275–80. New York: Wiley.

Masters, William H., and Virginia E. Johnson. 1970. *Human Sexual Inadequacy.* Boston: Little, Brown.

_____. 1979. *Homosexuality in Perspective.* Boston: Little, Brown.

Masters, William H., Virginia E. Johnson, and Robert C. Kolodny. 1985. *Human Sexuality,* 2d ed. Boston: Little, Brown.

McCall, George J., and J.L. Simmons. 1966. *Identities and Interactions: An Examination of Human Associations in Everyday Life.* New York: Free Press.

McDonald, Gary J. 1982. "Individual Differences in the Coming Out Process for Gay Men: Implications for Theoretical Models." *Journal of Homosexuality* 8(1): 47–60.

McIntosh, Mary. 1968. "The Homosexual Role." *Social Problems* 16(2): 182–92.

McKinney, Kathleen. 1985. "Ethical Issues and Dilemmas in the Teaching of the Sociology of Human Sexuality." *Quarterly Journal of Ideology* 9(4): 23–27.

McWhirter, David P., and Andrew M. Mattison. 1984. *The Male Couple: How Relationships Develop.* Englewood Cliffs, N.J.: Prentice-Hall.

Mead, George H. 1934. *Mind, Self, and Society.* Chicago: University of Chicago Press.

Meltzer, Bernard N. 1967. "Mead's Social Psychology." In *Symbolic Interaction: A Reader in Social Psychology,* edited by Jerome G. Manis and Bernard N. Meltzer, 5–24. Boston: Allyn & Bacon.

Meyer-Bahlburg, Heino F.L. 1977. "Sex Hormones and Male Homosexuality in Comparative Perspective." *Archives of Sexual Behavior* 6(4): 297–325.

_____. 1979. "Sex Hormones and Female Homosexuality: A Critical Examination." *Archives of Sexual Behavior* 8(2): 101-19.

_____. 1984. "Gender Development: Social Influences and Prenatal Hormone Effects. Introduction." *Archives of Sexual Behavior* 13(5): 391-93.

Mills, C. Wright. 1940. "Situated Actions and Vocabularies of Motive." *American Sociological Review* 5(6): 904-13.

Minton, Henry L., and Gary J. McDonald. 1983/1984. "Homosexual Identity Formation as a Developmental Process." *Journal of Homosexuality* 9(2/3): 91-104.

Money, John. 1985. "Gender: History, Theory and Usage of the Term in Sexology and Its Relationship to Nature/Nurture." *Journal of Sex and Marital Therapy* 11(2): 71-79.

"More Gay Men Choosing Celibacy and Monogamy." 1987. *Sexuality Today* 10(June 22): 2.

Omark, Richard. 1978a. "A Comment on the Homosexual Role." *Journal of Sex Research* 14(4): 273-74.

_____. 1978b. "On the Sexual Scripts of Gay Males and Lesbians." Paper presented at the annual meetings of the Association for Humanist Sociology, South Bend, Indiana.

_____. 1979. "On the Reification of Sexual Orientation Identity." Manuscript, University of Michigan, Flint.

_____. 1981a. "Further Comment on the Homosexual Role: A Reply to Goode." *Journal of Sex Research* 17(1): 73-75.

_____. 1981b. "Perspectives on the Homosexual Role and Gay Identity." Paper presented at the annual meetings of the Society for the Scientific Study of Sex, New York City.

"Partners and Practices Changing in the AIDS Era." 1986. *Sexuality Today* 10(October 20): 1.

Paul, Jay P. 1983/1984. "The Bisexual Identity: An Idea without Social Recognition." *Journal of Homosexuality* 9(2/3): 45-63.

_____. 1985. "Bisexuality: Reassessing Our Paradigms of Sexuality." *Journal of Homosexuality* 11(1/2): 21-34.

Plummer, Kenneth. 1975. *Sexual Stigma: An Interactionist Account.* London: Routledge & Kegan Paul.

_____. 1981a. "Going Gay: Identities, Life Cycles and Lifestyles in the Male Gay World." In *The Theory and Practice of Homosexuality,* edited by John Hart and Diane Richardson, 93-110. London: Routledge & Kegan Paul.

_____. 1981b. "Homosexual Categories: Some Research Problems in the Labeling Perspective of Homosexuality." In *The Making of the Modern Homosexual,* edited by Kenneth Plummer, 53-75. London: Hutchinson.

_____. 1984. "Sexual Diversity: A Sociological Perspective." In *The Psychology of Sexual Diversity,* edited by Kevin Howells, 219-53. New York: Basil Blackwell.

Ponse, Barbara. 1978. *Identities in the Lesbian World: The Social Construction of Self.* Westport, Conn.: Greenwood Press.

_____. 1980. "Lesbians and Their Worlds." In *Homosexual Behavior: A Modern Reappraisal,* edited by Judd Marmor, 157-75. New York: Basic Books.

_____. 1984. "The Problematic Meanings of Lesbian." In *The Sociology of Deviance,* edited by Jack D. Douglas, 25-33. Newton, Mass.: Allyn & Bacon.

Ponte, Meredith R. 1974. "Life in a Parking Lot: An Ethnography of a Homosexual Drive-In." In *Deviance: Field Studies and Self-Disclosures,* edited by Jerry Jacobs, 7-29. Palo Alto, Calif.: National Books.

Propper, Alice M. 1978. "Lesbianism in Female and Coed Correctional Institutions." *Journal of Homosexuality* 3(3): 265-74.

"Public Perceptions of Gays: Few Changes in Past Five Years." 1982. *Sexuality Today* 6(December 6): 1.

Rainwater, Lee. 1970. *Behind Ghetto Walls: Black Families in a Federal Slum.* Chicago: Aldine.

Reid, John. 1973. *The Best Little Boy in the World.* New York: Putnam.

Reinhart, Robert C. 1982. *A History of Shadows.* New York: Avon Books.

Reiss, Albert J. 1964. "The Social Integration of Peers and Queers." In *The Other Side,* edited by Howard S. Becker, 181–210. Glencoe, Ill.: Free Press.

Remafedi, Gary. "Male Homosexuality: The Adolescent's Perspective." *Pediatrics* 79(3): 326–30.

Richardson, Diane. 1981a. "Theoretical Perspectives on Homosexuality." In *The Theory and Practice of Homosexuality,* edited by John Hart and Diane Richardson, 5–37. London: Routledge & Kegan Paul.

_____. 1981b. "Lesbian Identities." In *The Theory and Practice of Homosexuality,* edited by John Hart and Diane Richardson, 111–24. London: Routledge & Kegan Paul.

_____. 1983/1984. "The Dilemma of Essentiality in Homosexual Theory." *Journal of Homosexuality* 9(2/3): 79–90.

Riddle, Dorothy I., and Stephen F. Morin. 1977. "Removing the Stigma: Data from Individuals." *APA Monitor* (November): 16, 28.

Ross, H. Laurence. 1971. "Modes.of Adjustment of Married Homosexuals." *Social Problems* 18(3): 385–93.

_____. 1972. "'Odd Couples': Homosexuals in Heterosexual Marriages." *Sexual Behavior* 1(7): 42–49.

Ross, Michael W. 1978. "The Relationship of Perceived Societal Hostility, Conformity, and Psychological Adjustment in Homosexual Males." *Journal of Homosexuality* 4(2): 157–68.

_____. 1980. "Retrospective Distortion in Homosexual Research." *Archives of Sexual Behavior* 9(6): 523–31.

Sagarin, Edward. 1973. "The Good Guys, the Bad Guys, and the Gay Guys." *Contemporary Sociology* 2(1): 3–13.

_____. 1975. "The Tyranny of 'Isness.'" In *Deviants and Deviance: An Introduction to the Study of Disvalued People and Behavior,* 144–54. New York: Praeger-Holt.

_____. 1976. "Thieves, Homosexuals and Other Deviants: The High Personal Cost of Wearing a Label." *Psychology Today* 9(10): 25–31.

_____. 1979. "Deviance without Deviants: The Temporal Quality of Patterned Behavior." *Deviant Behavior* 1(1): 1–13.

Saghir, Marcel T., and Eli Robins. 1973. *Male and Female Homosexuality: A Comprehensive Investigation.* Baltimore: Williams & Wilkins.

Schäfer, Siegrid. 1976. "Sexual and Social Problems among Lesbians." *Journal of Sex Research* 12(1): 50–69.

Scott, Marvin B., and Stanford M. Lyman. 1968. "Accounts." *American Sociological Review* 33(1): 46–62.

Sedlack, R. Guy, and Jay Stanley. 1984. "Research Methodology: The Interaction between Conceptualization and Empiricism." Manuscript, Towson State University.

"Sexuality Professionals Report Discrimination." 1985. *Sexuality Today* 8(September 23): 1.

Shively, Michael, and John P. De Cecco. 1978. "Components of Sexual Identity." *Journal of Homosexuality* 3(1): 41–48.

Siegelman, Marvin. 1972. "Adjustment of Male Homosexuals and Heterosexuals." *Archives of Sexual Behavior* 2(1): 9–25.

_____. 1979. "Adjustment of Homosexual and Heterosexual Women: A Cross-National Replication." *Archives of Sexual Behavior* 8(2): 101–19.

Simmons, J. L. 1965. "Public Stereotypes of Deviants." *Social Problems* 13(3): 223–32.

Simon, William, and John H. Gagnon. 1984. "Sexual Scripts." *Society* 22(1): 53–60.

Smith, Karen S. 1980. "Socialization, Identity, and Commitment: The Case of Female Homosexuals." Master's thesis, Miami University.

Socarides, Charles. 1970. "Homosexuality and Medicine." *Journal of the American Medical Association* 212(May 18): 1199–1202.

_____. 1972. "Homosexuality—Basic Concepts and Psychodynamics." *International Journal of Psychiatry* 10(1): 118–25.

_____. 1978. *Homosexuality*. New York: Jason Aronson.

Sophie, Joan. 1985/1986. "A Critical Examination of Stage Theories of Lesbian Identity Development." *Journal of Homosexuality* 12(2): 39–51.

Stanley, Julia Penelope, and Susan J. Wolfe, eds. 1980. *The Coming Out Stories*. Watertown, Mass.: Persephone Press.

Stone, Gregory P. 1962. "Appearance and the Self." In *Human Behavior and Social Processes,* edited by Arnold M. Rose, 86–118. Boston: Houghton-Mifflin.

Stone, Gregory P., and Harvey A. Farberman. 1970a. "The Self." In *Social Psychology through Symbolic Interaction,* edited by Gregory P. Stone and Harvey A. Farberman, 367–72. Waltham, Mass.: Xerox College Publishing.

_____. 1970b. "The Definition of the Situation." In *Social Psychology through Symbolic Interaction,* edited by Gregory P. Stone and Harvey A. Farberman, 147–53. Waltham, Mass.: Xerox College Publishing.

Strauss, Anselm L. 1969. *Mirrors and Masks*. San Francisco: Sociology Press.

Szasz, Thomas. 1970. *The Manufacture of Madness*. New York: Dell.

_____. 1980. *Sex by Prescription*. New York: Doubleday.

Tavris, Carol, and Carole Wade. 1984. *The Longest War: Sex Differences in Perspective*. 2d. ed. New York: Harcourt Brace Jovanovich.

Theodorson, George A., and Achilles G. Theodorson. 1969. *A Modern Dictionary of Sociology*. New York: Crowell.

Thompson, Norman L., Boyd R. McCandless, and Bonnie R. Strickland. 1971. "Personal Adjustment of Male and Female Homosexuals." *Journal of Abnormal Psychology* 78(2): 237–40.

Tourney, Garfield. 1980. "Hormones and Homosexuality." In *Homosexual Behavior: A Modern Reappraisal,* edited by Judd Marmor, 41–58. New York: Basic Books.

Travisano, Richard V. 1970. "Alternation and Conversion as Qualitatively Different Transformations." In *Sociology through Symbolic Interaction,* edited by Gregory P. Stone and Harvey A. Farberman, 594–605. Waltham, Mass.: Xerox College Publishing.

Troiden, Richard R. 1974. "Homosexual Encounters in a Highway Rest Stop." In *Sexual Deviance and Sexual Deviants,* edited by Erich Goode and Richard R. Troiden, 211–28. New York: Morrow.

_____. 1977. "Becoming Homosexual: Research on Acquiring a Gay Identity." Doctoral dissertation, SUNY-Stony Brook.

_____. 1979. "Becoming Homosexual: A Model of Gay Identity Acquisition." *Psychiatry* 42(4): 362–73.

_____. 1981. "Research as Process: The Human Dimension of Social Scientific Research." In *Readings for Social Research,* edited by Theodore C. Wagenaar, 108–18. Belmont, Calif.: Wadsworth.

_____. 1984/1985. "Self, Self-Concept, Identity, and Homosexual Identity: Constructs in Need of Definition and Differentiation." *Journal of Homosexuality* 10(3/4): 97–109.

Troiden, Richard R., and Erich Goode. 1980. "Variables Related to the Acquisition of a Gay Identity." *Journal of Homosexuality* 5(4): 383-92.

Van Wyk, Paul H. 1984. "A Critique of Dörner's Analysis of Hormonal Data from Bisexual Males." *Journal of Sex Research* 20(4): 412-14.

Ward, David A., and Gene G. Kassebaum. 1968. *Women's Prison: Sex and Social Structure.* Chicago: Aldine.

Warren, Carol A.B. 1972. "Identity and Community in the Gay World." Doctoral dissertation, University of Southern California.

_____. 1974. *Identity and Community in the Gay World.* New York: Wiley.

_____. 1980. "Homosexuality and Stigma." In *Homosexual Behavior: A Modern Reappraisal,* edited by Judd Marmor, 123-41. New York: Basic Books.

Warren, Carol A. B., and John M. Johnson. 1972. "A Critique of Labeling Theory from the Phenomenological Perspective." In *Theoretical Perspectives on Deviance,* edited by Robert A. Scott and Jack D. Douglas, 69-92. New York: Basic Books.

Warren, Carol A. B., and Barbara Ponse. 1977. "The Existential Self in the Gay World." In *Existential Sociology,* edited by Jack D. Douglas and John M. Johnson, 273-89. New York: Cambridge University Press.

Weeks, Jeffrey. 1981. "Discourse, Desire and Sexual Deviance: Some Problems in a History of Homosexuality." In *The Making of the Modern Homosexual,* edited by Kenneth Plummer, 76-111. London: Hutchinson.

Weinberg, Martin S., and Colin Williams. 1972. "Fieldwork among Deviants: Social Relations with Subjects and Others." In *Research on Deviance,* edited by Jack D. Douglas, 165-86. New York: Random House.

_____. 1974. *Male Homosexuals: Their Problems and Adaptations.* New York: Oxford University Press.

Weinberg, Thomas S. 1977. "Becoming Homosexual: Self-Disclosure, Self-Identity, and Self-Maintenance." Doctoral dissertation, University of Connecticut.

_____. 1978. "On 'Doing' and 'Being' Gay: Sexual Behavior and Homosexual Male Self-Identity." *Journal of Homosexuality* 4(2): 143-56.

Whitam, Frederick L. 1977a. "Childhood Indicators of Male Homosexuality." *Archives of Sexual Behavior* 6(2): 89-96.

_____. 1977b. "The Homosexual Role: A Reconsideration." *Journal of Sex Research* 13(1): 1-11.

_____. 1980. "The Prehomosexual Male Child in Three Societies: The United States, Guatemala, Brazil." *Archives of Sexual Behavior* 9(2): 87-99.

_____. 1981. "A Reply to Goode on the Homosexual Role." *Journal of Sex Research* 17(1): 66-72.

Whitam, Frederick L., and Robin M. Mathy. 1986. *Male Homosexuality in Four Societies: Brazil, Guatemala, the Philippines, and the United States.* New York: Praeger.

Whitam, Frederick L., and Michael Zent. 1984. "A Cross-Cultural Assessment of Early Cross-Gender Behavior and Familial Factors in Male Homosexuality." *Archives of Sexual Behavior* 13(5): 427-39.

Wolf, Timothy J. 1985. "Marriages of Bisexual Men." *Journal of Homosexuality* 11(1/2): 135-48.

Wolfgang, Marvin E., and Franco Ferracuti. 1967. *The Subculture of Violence.* London: Tavistock.

Wooden, Wayne S., and Jay Parker. 1982. *Men Behind Bars: Sexual Exploitation in Prison.* New York: Plenum.

Yankelovich, Daniel. 1974. *The New Morality: A Profile of American Youth.* New York: McGraw-Hill.

_____. 1981. *New Rules: Searching for Self-fulfillment in a World Turned Upside Down.* New York: Random House.

_____. 1984. "American Values: Change and Stability." *Public Opinion* 6(6): 2-9.

Zinik, Gary. 1985. "Identity Conflict or Adaptive Flexibility? Bisexuality Reconsidered." *Journal of Homosexuality* 11(1/2): 7-19.

ABOUT THE AUTHOR

Richard R. Troiden, an AASECT-certified Sex Educator and Sex Counselor, is Associate Professor of Sociology at Miami University (Ohio). He received his Ph.D. in Sociology from SUNY-Stony Brook in 1978. He is co-editor (with Erich Goode) of *Sexual Deviance and Sexual Deviants.* His current research interest (with Martin P. Levine) is on sexual addiction and compulsion.

Index